California Dreaming

California Dreaming

Society and Culture in the Golden State

EDITED BY
Ronald A. Wells

☞PICKWICK *Publications* · Eugene, Oregon

CALIFORNIA DREAMING
Society and Culture in the Golden State

Copyright © 2017 Wipf and Stock Publishers. All rights reserved. Except for brief quotations in critical publications or reviews, no part of this book may be reproduced in any manner without prior written permission from the publisher. Write: Permissions, Wipf and Stock Publishers, 199 W. 8th Ave., Suite 3, Eugene, OR 97401.

Pickwick Publications
An Imprint of Wipf and Stock Publishers
199 W. 8th Ave., Suite 3
Eugene, OR 97401

www.wipfandstock.com

PAPERBACK ISBN: 978-1-5326-0238-2
HARDCOVER ISBN: 978-1-5326-0240-5
EBOOK ISBN: 978-1-5326-0239-9

Cataloguing-in-Publication data:

Names: Wells, Ronald A., editor.

Title: California dreaming : society and culture in the golden state / edited by Ronald A. Wells.

Description: Eugene, OR: Pickwick Publications, 2017 | Includes bibliographical references.

Identifiers: ISBN 978-1-5326-0238-2 (paperback) | ISBN 978-1-5326-0240-5 (hardcover) | ISBN 978-1-5326-0239-9 (ebook)

Subjects: LCSH: California—History. | Religion and ethics—California. | California—Social life and customs. | Ethics.

Classification: LCC F861.5 C33 2017 (print) | LCC F861.5 (ebook)

Manufactured in the U.S.A.   09/08/17

This book is dedicated to the memory
of Kevin Owen Starr, 1940–2017.

He was the incomparable historian of California who
taught us to imagine "the California Dream." RIP.

Contents

Contributors | ix
Introduction | xi

The Enigma of California: Reflections on a Theological Subject | 1
—Richard J. Mouw

The Original Sin of California History: Race in California's "Founding Time" | 12
—Ronald A. Wells

"Let the Spirit Fly": Marilynn Kramar and the History of the Latino/a Catholic Charismatic Movement in the U.S.-Mexico Borderlands | 30
—Gaston Espinosa

Engaging Landscapes: San Francisco Bay Area Protestants in the Progressive Era | 53
—Douglas Firth Anderson

The Paradoxes of Life at the U.S.-Mexican Border: A View from Imperial County, California | 70
—Barbara A. Wells

Awakening the Desert and Harnessing the Colorado River: Power, Romance and the Ethics of Water in the Imperial Valley | 91
—Alicia Dewey

CONTENTS

Richard Henry Dana, Evangelical Consciousness, and the Colony of Hawiians in San Diego | 111

—RICK KENNEDY

Beating the Unbeatable Foe: Anti-Communism and Fear of Subversion in Southern Calfornia in the 1960s | 129

—WILLIAM KATERBERG

Contributors

Douglas Firth Anderson is Professor of History, Emeritus, Northwestern College, Iowa, where he continues as college Archivist.

Alicia Dewey is Associate Professor of History, Biola University, California.

Gaston Espinosa is Arthur V. Stoughton Professor of Religious Studies, Claremont McKenna College, California.

William Katerberg is Professor of History and Director of the Mellema Program in Western American Studies, Calvin College, Michigan.

Rick Kennedy is Professor of History, Point Loma Nazarene University, California.

Richard J. Mouw is President Emeritus, Fuller Theological Seminary, California, where he continues as Professor of Faith and Public Life.

Barbara A. Wells is Professor of Sociology, Vice-President and Academic Dean, Maryville College, Tennessee. She has been a Research Associate at the California Center for Border and Regional Economic Studies, San Diego State University—Imperial Valley.

Ronald A. Wells is Professor of History, Emeritus, Calvin College, Michigan. He is now Associate Director of the Maryville-Lee Symposium on Faith and the Liberal Arts, Maryville College, Tennessee.

Introduction

CALIFORNIA MATTERS, AS MUCH as a place as an idea. What famed historian Kevin Starr has called "the California Dream" is a vital part of American self-understanding.[1] The myth of California has it as follows: like America was meant to be a place of renewal, even redemption, for Europe, so California was to be a place of renewal for America. Therefore, California—place and idea—provides a fertile ground for scholars to think deeply about what it means to articulate "the promise of American life."

This book is presented in full awareness of the sea change in the context of North American intellectual life which has happened over the past forty years or so. Both as to subjects chosen for analysis and to the questions raised in the analysis, the vital new ingredient is the scholar's point of view. We now expect to hear diverse narratives about phenomena once thought to be settled facts that were told in a single voice, and in a way all well-intentioned scholars could understand. This change happened because of two parallel developments: post-modernism and the democratization of the academy.

Post-modernism is well known and many books have been written about it (e.g., Stanley Grenz, *A Primer on Post-Modernism*[2]). Briefly, post-modernism has undermined Enlightenment models of scientific detachment that had been cornerstones of the academy. Indeed, the motto of one of our most famous universities—*Veritas*—nowadays does not receive an affirmation but a question: "Truth—whose truth"?

The democratization of the academy has been an ally of post-modernism in this process because the academy now includes scholars from backgrounds that had been largely excluded. This is especially true for women and people of color. For example, a trio of very successful women scholars

---

1. *America and the California Dream* (New York: Oxford University Press, 1973)
2. (Grand Rapids: Eerdmans, 1996).

INTRODUCTION

stunned the intellectual world with a stinging rebuke. In *Telling the Truth and History*, Joyce Appleby, Lynn Hunt and Margaret Jacob wrote these memorable words: "We routinely, even angrily, ask: whose history? Whose science? Whose interests are being served by those ideas and those stories? The challenge is out to all claims of universality."[3] For these women to write about "telling the truth" does not mean that they think that prior historians were telling lies. That's exactly the point. We now no longer expect to find unitary versions of human phenomena; rather there are multiple representations of past and present realities. Those representations tell us a great deal about both the writer and the thing written about. This book takes its place in such an intellectual context.

Since this book is presented by scholars who are themselves people of faith, we would further establish our book's context by referring to the work of some of our colleagues who have contributed to the legitimation of the historian's perspective, both in choosing what subjects to research and in what questions to ask in that research. Perhaps the most outstanding example is the seminal work of George M. Marsden, who, in a group of books, has helped re-write both American religious history and how we might actually do history from a faith perspective. In his celebrated *The Outrageous Idea of Christian Scholarship*,[4] Marsden forthrightly argues two things: that people of faith indeed can do faith-based scholarship and that the academy need not unlearn all that it previously thought right. In short, because of the plurality of ideas that post-modernism allows, all honest scholars can have a seat at the table. Some historians have emphasized their "world views" in doing perspectival history.[5] Others have emphasized the notion of vocation that allows historians of faith to do their history faithfully.[6] Still others have used their own religious journeys as a starting place for their working toward a faithful historiography.[7]

---

3. (New York: Norton, 1977) 3.

4. (New York: Oxford University Press, 1998).

5. Ronald A. Wells, *History Through the Eyes of Faith* (San Francisco: HarperSanFrancisco, 1986); *History and the Christian Historian* (Grand Rapids: Eerdmans, 1998).

6. See especially, John Fea, *Confessing History: Explorations in Christian Faith and the Historian's Vocation* (South Bend, IN: Notre Dame University Press, 2010).

7. Mark Noll, *From Every Tribe and Nation: A Historian's Discovery of the Global Christian Story* (Grand Rapids: Baker, 2014); Margaret Bendroth, *The Spiritual Practice of Remembering* (Grand Rapids: Eerdmans. 2013).

INTRODUCTION

Finally, as to the intellectual background of the work presented here, we acknowledge the outstanding recent book by Jay Green.[8] The five versions of Christian historiography provide the outline for the book. They are: History that takes religion seriously; History seen through the lens of Christian faith commitments; History as applied ethics; History as Apologetics; History as a search for God. For this book, we find especially interesting Green's discussion of the ethical or moral aspects of faithful history. For historians like this, the intent of their work is to have moral impact on the reader. For historians on the Left, it means that history should incline towards social justice; to those on the Right it means to point to the right ordering of society on Christian principles, and most often a return to "Christian foundations." Jay Green agrees with the many historians he cites in his book that moral inquiry is a vital and unavoidable part of a properly-conceived Christian historiography. Most pointedly, and poignantly, Green quotes approvingly from historian David Harlan, about asking moral questions of the past: "This is what we value and want and don't yet have. This is how we mean to live and do not yet live."[9] For Green's part, he is cautious, and warns against going too full-bore towards moral inquiry, because historians are called to value the past on its own terms, not just as providing past examples to given instruction to the present. Nevertheless, he and the writers in the present book, agree that moral discourse is an important part of a faithful approach to history.

The chapters herein follow from what the authors see as moral discourse in their areas of interest. One comment about "morality" in this setting: we are not about ladling out praise and blame in some simplistic morality tale. Rather, these revisionist essays invite the reader to engage in a broader moral discourse about the California past and present in the context of each writer's concerns. Sometimes that engagement will be more explicit than in others, and sometimes more implied.

If Kevin Starr is right—and we think he is—that "the California Dream" is vital to "the American Mind," these essays are about important issues. If the present and the future is to be (in Starr's terms) renewed, even redeemed, then we all need to be "truthful," in the sense mentioned above, about our past(s). These essays are by no means meant to be the last word;

---

8. *Christian Historiography: Five Rival Versions* (Waco, TX: Baylor University Press, 2015).

9. *The Degradation of American History* (Chicago: University of Chicago Press, 1997) xxviii.

Introduction

but they are meant to join the conversation about what it means for people of good will, and with moral intent, to engage California.

The chapters in this book vary in terms of genre: thinking theologically about California, the religious history of certain groups and movements, a revisionist reading of a classic California novel, looking again at the morally contested founding time of California, the social history of water in the desert, listening to voices of women living near the border. The book, taken as a whole, represents what is exciting about writing history in the-time-after-the-modern. When, with Whitman, we "hear America singing" we hear different and diverse voices, coming from places not always represented in prior narratives, both secular and religious. We hope these essays shed new light on the California past, because California matters.

R.W.

Autumn 2016

The Enigma of California
Reflections on a Theological Subject

RICHARD J. MOUW

JOAN DIDION WAS BORN in Sacramento and has spent most of her life in California. In her memoir, *Where I Was from*, published in 2003, she tells us much about her many years of reflecting on what it means to be a Californian. The experience, she tells us, has not been a very pleasant one. "California," she confesses, "has remained in some ways impenetrable to me, a wearying enigma."[1]

Didion finds a kindred spirit in Josiah Royce, who left California in 1885 at age thirty to teach for the next three decades in Harvard's Philosophy Department. Like Didion, Royce also thought much about California. He wrote a book about California history, and he also reflected on his California origins in a speech that he gave in Philadelphia a few years before died. And also like Didion, he found the effort to understand his native state to be a difficult task. He testified that it had been a significant part of his "life's business" to try to understand the "wonder" of a California that encompasses both the "new" and the "crude."[2]

In thinking about California's "meaning," Didion and Royce are not only exploring their own connections to the state, but they are also trying to see beyond those personal ties to something bigger. What is that bigger something that they are looking for?

---

1. Joan Didion, *Where I Was from* (New York: Vintage, 2003) 38.

2. Ibid., 28–29. Didion's citation here of Royce is from "Words of Professor Royce at the Walton Hotel at Philadelphia, December 29, 1915," in Joseph K. Roh, ed., *The Philosophy of Josiah Royce* (New York: Crowell, 1971) 403.

California Dreaming

As a native of New Jersey I must confess that I have never given much thought to the subject of what the northern New Jersey of my youth "means." I suppose if I were forced to take up the project I could write ten pages or so about what it meant to grow up not far from the setting for Tony Soprano's escapades. I could say something, I think, about accents and modes of expression, about neighborhoods and their restaurants, and about having one's general outlook on life shaped by a daily exposure to diverse European immigrant communities.

For me, though, none of that would amount to much more than an exercise in nostalgia. I seriously doubt that I would have anything to offer that would interest readers eager to learn something about the "meaning" of New Jersey as such. Nor is New Jersey alone in its failure to evoke this kind of interest.

There are regions other than California, of course, that do seem to elicit more reflective explorations. The American South is an obvious case in point. Some of our best literature has explored the "meaning" of Southern roots—notable examples being *Uncle Tom's Cabin* and *The Adventures of Huckleberry Finn* on the fiction side, and the autobiographies of Frederick Douglass and Willie Morris in the non-fiction category.

What makes California and the South especially interesting is that each of those regions tells us something about the larger "meaning" of America, albeit in different ways. The respective food cultures illustrate at least one key difference. To describe Southern cooking is necessarily to look at history. It is to think about the different food sources of slaves and slave owners, about regional variations on the notion of what it means to be "barbeque," about the nuances of "Southern fried." California cuisine, on the other hand, is an ever-changing phenomenon—its enduring qualities are eclecticism and innovation.

To understand the South is to explore roots; it is to grasp traditions. To understand California is to monitor trends; the task requires a general surveying rather than a serious digging. And it is precisely because of this "surface" quality of what California stands for in many minds that it does not nurture the depth of belonging found among Southerners. Exiled Southerners, even when troubled by their native soil, often still feel an underlying affection, a sense of rootedness. Californians who set out to understand their regional culture's "meaning," on the other hand, often do so with a sense that there is much about that culture that they wish they could shake off. Thus Joan Didion's complaint that her California continues to be "impenetrable to me, a wearying enigma."

While Josiah Royce did not specifically address theological matters in focusing on California and its history, he did employ some biblical metaphors. The folks who ventured to the west coast around the time of the Gold Rush, he observes, were "going on a pilgrimage whose every suggestion was of the familiar sacred stories."[3] And for Royce, the pilgrims were for the most part on a *sinful* journey. They were, he says, "Jonahs" who "fled from before the word of the Lord" in order to seek "safety from their old vexatious duties in a golden paradise." And, arriving in California, they formed a "community of irresponsible strangers," an aggregate of "homeless" people, who "sought wealth, and not a social order."[4]

Not that Royce was consistently negative in his assessment of the Gold Rush generation. For all of the bad things that we might say about life in California's nineteenth-century mining towns, Royce observes, we can also discern on occasion a healthy desire for a shared sense of community. "Mutual strangers" banded together, he says, with an observable "willingness to compromise on matters in dispute," accompanied by "the desire to be in public on pleasant terms with everybody."[5]

Royce's insistence on seeing some good things at work in the early shaping of California's culture gets at something that is theologically important. He has exercised a kind of cultural discernment, identifying some positive forces at work in the early shaping of the culture of California.

David Tiede, the former president of Luther Seminary, once made a memorable observation in a devotional he gave to a group of academic administrators. The crude and even blasphemous language of the streets, he said, often contains theological meanings that the speakers are oblivious to. His two examples were: "What *in the hell* is going on?!" and "What *in heaven's name* is happening?!" These two expressions, Tiede said, get at important spiritual realities: there is a lot of hellish stuff going on in the world;

---

3. Josiah Royce, *California, From the Conquest in 1846 to the Second Vigilance Committee in San Francisco: A Study of American Character* (Boston: Houghton Mifflin, 1886) 246.

4. Ibid., 274–75.

5. Ibid., 280.

but we can also on occasion discern things that draw, even if unwittingly, upon heavenly resources.

Josiah Royce was allowing for a bit of the heavenly amidst much of the hellishness of nineteenth-century mining camp life in California. And it is good for us, as we think in a more sustained theological manner about California's "meaning," to follow his lead. To be sure, I am suggesting that in doing so we honor what for me is an explicitly Calvinist impulse—at least in the "Kuyperian" version of Calvinism. The late Mennonite theologian John Howard Yoder once captured the nature of this impulse quite nicely when, in the course of one of our public Anabaptist-Calvinist debates in the 1970s, he responded to a question from the audience with this comment: on questions of culture, he observed, "Mouw wants to say, 'Fallen, but *created*,' and I want to say, 'Created, but *fallen*.'"

My approach to California's "meaning," then, views the fallenness of the Golden State as a perversion of an original createdness. The general point was put nicely by H. Richard Niebuhr when, in his endorsement of the "Christ transforming culture" approach, Niebuhr argues that human culture as we presently experience it is "corrupted order rather than order for corruption . . . It is perverted good, not evil; or it is evil as perversion, and not as badness of being."[6]

This applies nicely, I think, to California. It is always relevant and important to ask these two questions about things that we observe in the California experience: What hellishness is at work here? And what might we be seeing that honors the heavenly?

A Southern California couple were talking recently about a two-week visit, from Oklahoma, of their twenty-something granddaughter. "She would love to move here," the grandparents reported. "She just feels that so much is *happening* here, and she wants to find it."

Josiah Royce used the quest motif in explaining the motives of the Gold Rush generation, and it applies equally to the young woman from Oklahoma. Nor is her quest necessarily a bad thing. We are driven by quests as human beings. In the words of Augustine's oft quoted prayer at the

---

6. H. Richard Niebuhr, *Christ and Culture* (New York: Harper & Row, 1951) 194.

beginning of the *Confessions*: "Thou hast made us for thyself and restless is our heart until it comes to rest in thee."[7]

California is an arena for human restlessness—and very often that restlessness is misdirected. And while the restlessness associated with California is a manifestation of a more general human restlessness, we can safely say that the way in which California manages both to attract and to encourage human restlessness stands out in the broader American culture.

A young Silicon Valley venture capitalist put it well to me not long ago. One of his leisure time activities, following through on a history course he had taken as an undergraduate, is studying twelfth- and thirteenth-century medieval thought, with a focus on the uses made of Aristotle's metaphysics. When I asked him why this interest, he said: "I guess it has to do with the speed of life when you are constantly involved with start-ups. You lose a sense of being a self that has a history. I have to keep working at being connected to something in the past!"

This person is taking definite steps to protect himself from a threat to selfhood that he sees as somehow intrinsic to the preoccupations and pace of his life. He is describing the way in which life in Silicon Valley can be its own version of a surfing culture: a skimming across surfaces without a proper connection to anything stable beneath those surfaces. Albert Borgmann, a Roman Catholic who teaches philosophy at the University of Montana, wrote an excellent book a few years ago in which he discusses the ways in which the postmodern consciousness often limits its attention to the *surfaces* of reality. He addresses this malady with a call to rediscover "the eloquence of things" in their particularity, to recognize "the things that command our respect and grace our life," thus finding "the depth of the world."[8]

We can generalize here on the images we applied to California cuisine: innovation and eclecticism. California means innovative drawing together from diverse sources. This produces much that is good—there is much to thank God for in what we have received from Silicon Valley. But the resulting way of life can sometimes become a surface thing, lacking depth, an absence of rootedness.

---

7. http://www.fordham.edu/halsall/basis/confessions-bod.html/.

8. Albert Borgmann, *Crossing the Postmodern Divide* (Chicago: University of Chicago Press, 1992) 51, 82.

Much of this territory is covered with considerable insight by Monica Ganas in her important book, *Under the Influence: California's Intoxicating Spiritual and Cultural Impact on America*. She approaches her topic with a trained cultural eye: she worked for several decades in the entertainment industry before taking up her teaching role in theater, film and communication studies at Azusa Pacific University. Drawing on all of this, she provides a wealth of illuminating cultural information and perspective, both historical and contemporary, including some wonderful personal anecdotes. And best of all, she deals with the complexity of California life out of strongly stated Christian convictions, with many theological and missiological insights.

Ganas sets the stage for her discussion with a clear distinction between the hellish and the heavenly. On the one hand, she says, there is "the delusional and damaging effects of *California-as-a-contrived-religion*"; but there is also, beneath all of the damage, "the promise of *California-the-created-region*." At work in all of the sordid patterns of California life, she says, there are "eternal instincts and longings" that point to "redemptive possibilities." These created yearnings can, if properly redirected, help us to "turn our attention to our real environment, real community, real relationships, and real policies." Without that redirecting, though, we will find ourselves in a trance-like state that "anesthetizes us to actual human experience, relationship, environment, and, I fear, the true God."[9]

Ganas's book contributes much to the project of thinking theologically about California. But she sometimes—and I stress sometimes—seems to push things in a direction that makes me nervous, and I think the nervousness is worthy of some theological explication.

I began to experience a little discomfort early on in Ganas's book, when she employed the "empire" image, as set forth in Walter Brueggemann's stark contrast between Christ's Kingdom and our human-created empires. Here is her summary of the contrast:

> The kingdom is based on grace, the empire on earnings. The kingdom is freeing, the empire binding. The kingdom is peaceful, the empire brutal. The kingdom is authentic, the empire deceitful. The kingdom is forgiving, the empire judgmental. The kingdom is renewing, the empire debilitating. The kingdom is imaginative, the empire predictable. The kingdom is filled with second chances

---

9. Monica Ganas, *Under the Influence: California's Intoxicating Spiritual and Cultural Impact on America* (Grand Rapids: Brazos, 2010) 4, 5.

and good news to the poor. The empire is filled with power, greed, and injustice.[10]

I have no difficulty with this kind of contrast as such. We do, of course, wrestle, not so much against flesh and blood in California, but against principalities and powers. We run into problems, however, when we simply identify the actual realities of California culture—it's very real "flesh and blood"—with these "empire" characteristics. Indeed, I see the danger here as closely associated with the "empire" talk as such. Empires range over territories and take much of their shape in institutional realities. I think it is misleading to think of Calfornia's cultural "territory" as a part of "empire" in that sense.

Back in the 1970s, some of my friends in the evangelical activist movement were taken—particularly in our opposition to the Vietnam war—with the kind of rhetoric set forth by William Stringfellow, who depicted the United States as Revelation's sinful Babylon, embodying and promoting a global "way of death."[11] As a parent in those days of a young child just starting school, I found this depiction difficult to reconcile with my son's daily walking route to and from his inner-city school. Along the way there were stop signs and traffic signals, and at one key point a uniformed crossing guard. His school was regularly visited by fire and safety inspectors. All of these things were life-promoting gifts. There was much that I wanted to criticize in those days about "the American way"—and there still is today. But to characterize it as a "way of death," or as in the more recent rhetoric, an "empire" that is devoted to what is "brutal" and "deceitful" and "debilitating," is to fail to recognize the life-affirming gifts that it makes available to us.

And this shows up in other areas of contemporary life. For example, when I have stayed in European hotels I have often missed the "customer service" orientation that strikes me as typical in California hotels. It's nice to be welcomed by a desk clerk, and to receive a call from her a few minutes later, in the assigned room, asking whether the room is satisfactory. I have no doubt that the display of California friendliness is mandated by a corporate culture that has made decisions about the profitability of "customer satisfaction." But, then, I am not asking to be loved—only to have a fairly comfortable stay for a night or two away from home.

---

10. Ganas, *Under the Influence*, 13–14.

11. William Stringfellow, *An Ethics for Christians and Other Aliens in a Strange Land* (Waco, TX: Word, 1973).

That there is more at stake here than our terminological preferences can be seen in Ganas's account of the continuing legacy of California's Gold Rush. "True to gold rush form," she writes, the contemporary person who is intoxicated by California "is still looking out for number one, still staking claims, corporately and individually, whether in traffic jams or grocery lines or crowded gyms or sales bins or church pews. We're still eyeing our neighbor suspiciously, still on guard against the foreign element, which can be anyone who threatens our space."[12] What is missing here is the kind of concession that we saw Royce making about the Gold Rush. He gave us some reason to think of at least some of what went on in nineteenth-century mining towns as more like Brueggemann's depiction of Christ's Kingdom than of the rebellious patterns of "empire" sinfulness.

This applies to busy streets in school districts and hotel lobbies as well. And, I must add in this context, it applies to movie theaters. Monica Ganas knows much about the film industry, and her book offers many insights on that important area of California culture. But there are times when I fear that she is too captivated by the notion that somehow the film industry simply is "in" the "empire." Here, for example, is Ganas describing the way we can be tempted to see ourselves as "omniscient and omnipresent" while watching a film:

> Sitting in the hushed darkness of the film cathedral, enjoying our sacramental popcorn for which we've paid too high a price, congregants gaze at the altar of the screen and are given plot information that many characters in the movie do not know and cannot control. We piece together the story we are told, traveling from location to location with or without all the characters, filling in the narrative gaps, and thus it begins to feel as though we ourselves are telling the story. It seems to be our own idea, and thus difficult to refute for the time being, whether or not it aligns with our general beliefs.

All of this is enhanced, she says, by the use of "powerful enough technologies to insure the success of this mystical enterprise." Special effects and the like can invite us into an intimacy with characters who become, Ganas observes, "larger than life," thereby "lend[ing] a supernatural component to the action and serve to mak[ing] the narrative at least as vital as the one we're hearing at church."[13]

---

12. Ganas, *Under the Influence*, 62.
13. Ibid., 77–78.

I have at least two concerns about this kind of depiction. One is that while making a film—and watching one—can indeed be a grasping at omniscience and omnipotence, and thus yet one more way of taking up the Tempter's challenge that we "can be like God"—while I do think it *can* be that, I do not think it *must* be. The very things Ganas points to as potential instruments of rebellion against God can also serve the cause of righteousness, functioning, for example, as effective tools of moral—and even spiritual—pedagogy. Allowing us to see plot patterns and connections that the characters in the film themselves cannot see—and seeing them "larger than life"—can be a way of alerting us to a narrative unity that provides an alternative, by filling in temporal and spatial gaps, to what would otherwise be a fragmented plot-line.

More importantly for me, though, is my uneasiness with Ganas's use of church-going imagery: the picture of the theater as a "film cathedral" that dispenses "sacramental popcorn," with "congregants gaz[ing] at the altar of the screen," and all of this in the service of a "mystical enterprise."

My worry about this kind of thing was captured nicely by Mark Galli in a *Books & Culture* review essay dealing with writers who are fond of depicting football games and other major sports events in religious categories, as when the Super Bowl becomes a ritualized event that produces ecstasy, creating bonding experiences, fostering communal celebrations, calling for "physical sacrifice," and so forth. Galli rightly rejects such portrayals of a football game as such. Certainly there are many people, he writes, for whom "football has become an idol. Such is the nature of the human heart, that desperately wicked thing (Jer. 17: 9)." But it is precisely because many of us experience true religion that we can relax and see a football game for what it is: one of the places where we can often see God's "handiwork and love" being manifested.[14] When that happens, we can be grateful for amazing eighty-yard runs, spectacular pass receptions, and a coach's wise use of time-outs in the final minutes of the game. The old anti-Freudian remark that sometimes a cigar is just a cigar has its parallel here. Sometimes a football game is just a football game. And sometimes eating popcorn at a good movie is just eating popcorn at a good movie.

This is not to deny, of course, that there can very well be—and often is—bad football games and bad popcorn and bad movies. And there are indeed cases where football and popcorn and movies can function in obvious ways as "empire"—because they have become instruments of deceit and

---

14. Mark Galli, "And God Created Football," *Books & Culture* (2010) 9–10.

destruction. But sometimes the badness is of a less cosmic sort: the game is poorly played by both teams. Or the popcorn is stale or much too salty. Or the film's special effects render certain key scenes ineffective.

Much the same holds for the state of California. In many aspects of its life, California is simply a region where many very ordinary things happen on a daily basis: people search for parking spaces, couples get married, writers struggle with finding just the right opening paragraph, and parents are pleased that their teenage daughter got a summer job selling popcorn in the local movie complex.

Sometimes too—often, in fact, in our sinful world—much of this goes bad, as when people fight in parking lots, or when the caterer messes up the food for the wedding reception, or the writer decides to get the readers' attention with a lurid description, or the teenager falls in with the wrong crowd at her summer job selling popcorn.

And sometimes California as a general reality also goes horribly bad, as when it presents itself as a "Golden State" that lures us into false hopes of an earthly paradise of freewheeling self-actualizers who are liberated from the inhibitions that characterize life in other regions. When that happens, at least some of the language associated with an "empire" ideology may shed light on California's wicked ways.

But in all of that it is important to remind ourselves that the Creator— to use a wonderful hymn line that I chose as a title for one of my books, "shines in all that's fair." This is where I find Abraham Kuyper's theology so helpful. Common grace, for Kuyper, is a non-salvific manifestation of divine favor toward the fallen creation. In good part it is a restraining grace, a "leash" on sinfulness that keeps human beings from being as bad as they could be. But it also works positively in unredeemed life. Kuyper sees common grace at work in a positive manner "wherever civic virtue, a sense of domesticity, natural love, the practice of human virtue, the improvement of the public conscience, integrity, mutual loyalty among people, and a feeling for piety leaven life."[15]

The danger of an "empire" approach to the study of California as a complex cultural phenomenon is that it might keep us from noticing those very signs of common grace. Ganas is right to sensitize us both to "the delusional and damaging effects of *California-as-a-contrived-religion*" and to "the promise of *California-the-created-region*." To look for the damage

---

15. Abraham Kuyper, "Common Grace," in James D. Bratt, ed., *Abraham Kuyper: A Centennial Reader* (Grand Rapids: Eerdmans, 1998) 181.

is important. But so is the effort to discern the signs of promise. To miss them is to be left with nothing more than a California that is Joan Didion's "wearying enigma."

The Original Sin of California History

Race in California's "Founding Time"

Ronald A. Wells

In recent years I have been interested in certain concerns that center on an essential question best expressed by the title of a book to which I contributed a chapter: *The Politics of Past Evil*.[1] In that book a group of scholars asked how societies and peoples that had experienced violence and civil discord were able to work through the conflicts of the past—and differing memories of them—in order to move forward to peace. Part of the answer lies in the ability of one or both communities in the historic conflict to make confession for past wrongs.

In this chapter I revisit "the conquest" of the American West. We are helped to focus our re-evaluation by using the seminal work of the historian and moral philosopher, Josiah Royce. His classic work, published in 1886, has a long nineteenth-century title that no scholar would use today: *California, From the Conquest in 1846 to the Second Vigilance Committee in San Francisco: A Study of American Character* [hereafter we will simply call it *California*]. It gives us an insight into the way in which conflicted histories can be negotiated and "the politics of past evil" can be addressed. Royce's work also is vital because it anticipates the work of the most important and influential historian of the American frontier, Frederick Jackson Turner. In short, Royce's moral history of the conquest offers us today a kind of case

---

1. Daniel Philpott, ed., *The Politics of Past Evil: Religion, Reconciliation and the Dilemmas of Transitional Justice* (Notre Dame: University of Notre Dame Press, 2006).

study of how history can be redeemed if we put alternate stories, confession and justice as the central concerns.

It might be well to identify this "past evil," this "original sin" of California history; it centers on racism. Recently Jim Wallis named racism as the sin of all American history. Richard Rodriquez called it America's "founding sin."[2] But, a generation earlier Kevin Starr used the term "original sin" in California history, in which he referenced Josiah Royce's work,

All work on California history must acknowledge in some way the celebrated multi-volume history of the state by the eminent historian, Kevin Starr. He devotes a chapter to Josiah Royce in the first volume of the series. In *Americans and the California Dream* Starr sees Royce as much a figure *in* California history as a key early interpreter *of* California history.[3] We will refer to Starr and his work several times below.

The Importance of Josiah Royce's *California* for Our Time

In the mid-1980s two books appeared that were important in re-orienting public discourse about the past and the future of American life: Robert Bellah's *Habits of the Heart*[4] and Patricia Nelson Limerick's *The Legacy of Conquest*[5] Later, two groups of scholars evaluated these books, and the authors were given an opportunity for response. In both cases the celebrated authors wrote of their own surprise in acknowledging that they had had a nineteenth-century scholar in the back of their minds when writing their books but had not said so. They both stated their previously unacknowledged debt to Josiah Royce.

In *Habits of the Heart*, Robert Bellah and his colleagues reached back to that incomparable observer of America—Alexis de Tocqueville—to discuss what the core American belief in individualism had done to American values and beliefs. When a noted group of Catholic scholars critiqued

---

2. Jim Wallis, *America's Original Sin: Racism, White Privilege and the Bridge to a New America* (Grand Rapids: Brazos, 2016). Richard Rodriquez, *Brown: The Last Discovery of America* (New York: Penguin, 2003).

3. Kevin Starr, *America and the California Dream* (New York: Oxford University Press, 1973).

4. Robert Bellah et al., *Habits of the Heart: Individualism and Commitment in American Life* (Berkeley: University of California Press, 1984).

5. Patricia Nelson Limerick, *The Legacy of Conquest: The Unbroken Past of the American West* (New York: Norton, 1987).

Habits, and one of them suggested the salience of Josiah Royce to the discussion about individualism and community,[6] Bellah responded:

> I was embarrassed to discover that our own memory had lapsed in that the authors of *Habits* did not credit Royce with the terms "community of memory" and "community of hope" which play a central role in our argument. Royce was in the background of several of us but we did not return to him in the period when we were writing *Habits*.[7]

In *Legacy of Conquest*, Patricia Nelson Limerick accomplished a signal success in collapsing the intellectual world given us by Frederick Jackson Turner, who had seen a discontinuity between the culture-shaping time of the "frontier" and our own time. Rather, Limerick insisted, there were and are fundamental continuities between that time and ours, in terms of race, ethnicity, gender and economics. But, when Limerick reflected on her work two years after the book's publication[8]—in the context of an evaluation of *Legacy* by a blue-ribbon group of scholars—she admitted some "failings" in *Legacy*: "Perhaps most embarrassing [was] the unacknowledged, uncited status of Josiah Royce. In a number of ways, *Legacy* is an argument for awarding Royce his deserved status as the father of western history."[9]

The purpose here is not to fault Bellah and Limerick. But, one observes that when two prominent intellectuals write important books, and later they were "embarrassed" not to have acknowledged their debts to Josiah Royce, we know we are on to something worthwhile about the importance of Royce's work for our own time.

As we seek, with Kevin Starr and others, to sort out the various meanings for us of the California founding time, we do well to listen again to a writer who combined criticism of, and admiration for, what was to become "the California dream" in the American mind. Our re-reading of a classic text like Royce's can help us in the project of morally reconstructing American memory.

---

6. Frank M. Oppenheim, "A Roycean Response to the Challenge of Individualism," Donald L. Gelpi, ed., *Beyond Individualism: Toward A Retrieval of Moral Discourse in America* (Notre Dame: University of Notre Dame Press, 1989) 87–119.

7. Quoted in Gelpi, ed., *Beyond Individualism*, 222

8. Donald Worster et al., "The Legacy of Conquest by Patricia Nelson Limerick: A Panel of Appraisal," *Western Historical Quarterly*, 20 (1989) 303–22.

9. Ibid., 317.

Josiah Royce's *California . . . A Study of American Character*

Josiah Royce, then a young instructor at Harvard University, published in 1886 what was among the first serious histories of California. It is the kind of history one might expect from a moral philosopher. Moreover, it presages by a century our concerns with the whole genre of studies on history and memory, which is what makes it so fascinating. Royce had not intended to be a historian of California. He was chosen for the assignment not because he was an academically-trained historian of California but because he was available through Harvard connections and because he was a native Californian. He was to make a major name for himself as a moral philosopher, teaching at Harvard for thirty years and writing more than a score of books and many articles in philosophy. While it is his role as historian that interests us here, we cannot take Royce's historical work out of the context of his larger efforts in philosophy.[10]

Though not trained in history Royce did his research and writing with the concerns of a scholar, with meticulous attention to detail and documentation. In fact, he later told a friend that writing history was much more difficult than writing philosophy because in history one had to stick to the facts.[11] Not only did he think and write like a scholar he had the good fortune of having had nearly unlimited access to the library of Hubert Howe Bancroft. That library was to be the foundation for the Bancroft Library at the University of California. He is credited for later writing, along with his assistants, the monumental achievement of a multi-volume history of California, matched only in our time by the magisterial work of Kevin Starr. Royce finished his more limited book before Bancroft, and he gave Bancroft

---

10. For biographies of Royce, see especially John Clendenning, *The Life and Thought of Josiah Royce* (Madison: University of Wisconsin Press, 1985; rev. ed., Nashville: Vanderbilt University Press, 1999); the most accessible is Robert V. Hine, *Josiah Royce: From Grass Valley to Harvard* (Norman: University of Oklahoma Press, 1992). In recent years there has been a revival of interest in Royce, and even a scholarly society about his work. See especially Kelly Parker, ed., *Josiah Royce for the Twenty-First Century: Historical, Ethical, and Religious Interpretations* (Lanham, MD: Lexington, 2012); Kelly Parker, *The Relevance of Royce* (New York: Fordham University Press, 2014). Other recent, good scholarly works on Royce that are worthy of note include: Jacquelyn Ann Kegley, *Josiah Royce in Focus* (Bloomington: Indiana University Press, 2008); Douglas R. Anderson, *Philosophy Americana* (New York: Fordham University Press, 2008) esp. 33–49.

11. Letter, Royce to Henry L. Oak, September 17, 1885, in *Letters of Josiah Royce*, ed. John Clendenning (Chicago: University of Chicago Press, 1970) 178.

full credit in *California*. In sum, Royce was not only good as a scholar, he was lucky as a researcher to have Bancroft's help. Moreover, he was unique in being the first scholar, lucky or otherwise, to write on the state who was himself a native Californian. He brought an intuitive feel to the subject, and a passion born out of his desire to see the moral significance of the "new land" of his birth. He was also unique in another respect: in researching *California* Royce asked his mother to write her memoirs of being a forty-niner, which she probably would not have written without her son's request. Because of it, Royce wrote a better book and we have one of the best accounts of pioneer life from a woman's perspective. A generation later, Yale-historian Ralph Henry Gabriel edited and introduced what Sarah Bayliss Royce had called her "Pilgrimage Journey."[12]

Royce's sense for early California life was born out of a deep curiosity about his native town, Grass Valley, which was itself only about half-dozen years older than Royce. His early experiences in the Sierra Nevada were to fill him with wonder about the nature of society itself:

> My earliest recollections include a very frequent wonder as to what my elders meant when they said this was a new community. I frequently looked at the vestiges left by the former diggings of miners, saw that many pine logs were rotten, and that a miner's grave was to be found in a lonely place not far from my own house. Plainly men had lived and died thereabouts ... The logs and graves looked old. The sunsets were beautiful. The wide prospects when one looked across the Sacramento Valley were impressive and had long interested the people of whose love for my country I heard much. What was there then in this place that ought to be called new, or for that matter, crude? I wondered, and gradually came to feel that part of my life's business was to find out what all this wonder meant.[13]

It was from an early age, he later recalled, that is ideas about the nature of persons and society in community were formed: "I strongly feel that my deepest motives and problems have centered about the Idea of the Community, although this idea has only gradually come into my consciousness. This was what I was intensely feeling, in the days when my sisters and I looked across the Sacramento Valley, and wondered about the great world

---

12. *A Frontier Lady: Recollections of the Gold Rush and Early California*, ed. Ralph Henry Gabriel (New Haven: Yale University Press, 1932).

13. *The Hope of the Great Community* (New York: Macmillan, 1916) 5.

beyond our mountains."[14] The "great world" would, of course, be very large indeed under the scrutiny of this mind of colossal energy. But, he always tried to balance the particular and the universal, or, as he was later to say, the provincial and the great community.

Royce's personal interest in the history of California was lifelong. Although he did not write professionally about California after 1891, the whole of his philosophical work was part his working out the failure of, and the need for, community in his native California. For Royce the philosopher, abstract ideas came to life in the realities of life as lived. As he developed philosophical positions on what he called "loyalty," "provincialism" "the beloved community," California was never far from Royce's mind. If there was one single point to be distilled from Royce's *California* and from his other work, it is that humans cannot escape social duties. As Patricia Nelson Limerick was later to write in *Legacy of Conquest*, "The cruel but common lesson of western history: postponements and evasions catch up with people."[15]

I have read all of Royce's writings on California. I have also read his personal letters in manuscript form in the archives at Harvard University and the University of California at Berkeley, some of which were later collected and published by John Clendenning.[16] His writings and his letters, taken together, reveal a man who may have begun his work on California in a relatively light-hearted spirit, possibly unaware of the enormity of the task ahead; but they also reveal a person who matured as a scholar and a moral observer of society in the process. In the story of California he saw the triumph that others had seen, but saw tragedy too; he saw the heroism that other writers saw, but treachery too; he joined with others in celebrating the best in American character as shown in early California, but he also saw the worst, and was unafraid to say so. Because he could get past simple polarities about the moral aspects of early California life, Royce received much criticism, as he engaged in a bitter battle for historical truth concerning the years 1846–1856.

What strikes one in reading Royce's *California* and his many journalistic pieces in the battle of words that followed the book's publication, is his responsible, careful and nuanced writing, as compared to what his letters indicate of how he really felt about it. His letters reveal a person who is

---

14. Ibid.
15. *Legacy of Conquest*, 95.
16. *The Letters of Josiah Royce* (Chicago: University of Chicago Press, 1970).

shocked, even appalled at times, both by the story of early California history itself, but even more so by the attempted cover-up of odious aspects by the participants and their descendants. There was also the problem of the historical record being willfully distorted or muted, either by the historical actors themselves, or more typically by relatives and friends who wished to portray a decent, even heroic, past when dispute and dishonor also needed to be admitted. Royce was a moral social analyst who decried injustice. Moreover, he became downright angry with those who lied about, and tried to cover up, the injustices they had perpetrated.

Some subsequent scholars, even those sympathetic to Royce, believe he overdid it, both in terms of his verbosity and of his seemingly relentless, some would say obsessive, pursuit of the legend of John C. Frémont. As to the first point, any modern reader would question Royce on his verbiage. Where one word would do, he used two. It seems he was the same way in person. If one asked Royce a question, all the available space was filled by the answer, leaving some questioners sorry they had asked.[17] Royce was nothing if not thorough; but he seems not to have mastered the difference between thoroughness and verbosity. Thus, we are not alone in seeking Royce's wisdom in a leaner form. But the other charge, that Royce went way over the top in his pursuit of Frémont is not so easy to concede. In the end, I think we must sympathize with Royce; even if he wrote too much on the Frémont legend, that legend, as Royce lamented, would not go down, despite the facts of the case. This chapter, then, risks joining Royce in possible over-emphasis on the Frémont affair; but since it is crucial—both to later interpreters of California and to Royce's credibility in our eyes—we must follow this up.

We will detail below some of the pertinent facts relating to the Frémont controversy, but for now a few words will suffice. Captain John C. Frémont, a well-known explorer, was in California in 1845-46. When the hostilities of the Mexican War began to impinge on California, Frémont associated himself with a group of Americans along the Sacramento River who were restive under Mexican control, and "The Bear Flag" revolt began. The question, in 1846 and when Royce wrote forty years later, was this: on what orders did Frémont act? Since the policy of the United States was to welcome the *Californios* [who Royce calls the native Californians], not antagonize them, "the conquest" set in place an unfortunate pattern of racial-ethnic relations in California that was difficult to overcome. Royce,

---

17. Clendenning, *Life and Thought*, 330–31.

as a moral philosopher, deplored that pattern. The Frémont legend was, and is, vital to California history: if Frémont was right, that he acted on orders, then Californians must rightly regard him as their hero; if he had no orders, and his actions poisoned ethnic relations, then he is the villain in the piece. Frémont was, after all, the first Republican candidate for president, and he had a considerable reputation, based on his early California career.

When Josiah Royce began his research for California in the summer of 1884, he had access to Bancroft's unique library of documents, memoirs and newspapers. It soon became obvious to Royce that things did not look good for Frémont. But, cautious and scholarly, Royce wondered if there was an alternative interpretation than what seemed to be developing in his mind. As it turned out, a mutual friend of his from Berkeley undergraduate days, and also a distant relative of Frémont—William Jones—agreed to set up an interview between Royce and Frémont. He sent Jones the sorts of questions he wanted to ask [by then, General] Frémont. Royce was deferential, saying that he need not even bother the aged hero if documentary evidence could be point to that would satisfy Royce's questions.[18] They preferred an interview, which occurred in early December, 1884 at the Frémont home in New York.

Royce spoke with General Frémont and his wife, Jessie, the daughter of Senator Thomas Hart Benton, who had been a prominent figure in antebellum politics. Because of Royce's access to Bancroft's documents, he had obtained a copy of an 1846 dispatch from Secretary of State Buchanan to Thomas Larkin, the American consul at Monterey in the 1840s. The document was vitally important because it disclosed both the American policy in California and who was in charge of it. The policy of the Polk Administration was clearly designed to bring California into the Union, but Larkin was to ensure the harmony of that desire with the good feelings of the *Californios*. Larkin, then, was the government's secret agent in California, not Frémont, and the policy was "peaceful persuasion" toward the Mexican population.

During the interview, Royce kept quiet about the Larkin dispatch in his pocket. The Frémont's insisted that no such dispatch existed and that Larkin could never have been trusted by Polk for such a delicate assignment. They insisted that Frémont was the government's man in California.[19] A

---

18. Letter, Royce to Jones, September 23, 1884, Jones papers, Bancroft Library, Berkeley. Hereinafter letters will be noted by collection and "Berkeley."

19. Letter, Royce to Henry L. Oak, December 9, 1884, *Letters*, 141–45.

California Dreaming

biographer of Frémont will not directly admit that Royce had the goods on Frémont; rather he chose to attack Royce. Regarding the infamous "Larkin dispatch," the biographer writes that "Royce perversely did not reveal that had copied such a telltale document."[20] While there is little doubt in Royce's written account of the interview that he thoroughly enjoyed catching the great "pathfinder" lying, keeping silent does not necessarily reveal perversity but caution. Royce realized two things: that if a young scholar tried to deconstruct the Frémont legend it would occasion stiff opposition, so he had to be careful; and, part of that care was to verify his documents. The one he had in his pocket was a copy of one of Bancroft's copies. He believed he needed to see the original before going public with it.

In the early spring of 1885, Royce made a quick research trip to Washington, D.C. He went to the State department, and after some negotiations over what today we would call "national security issues," Royce was able to see the original "Larkin dispatch." By mid-April 1885, Royce knew what he had to do. On April 14, he wrote his publisher, Horace Scudder, and a key assistant in the Bancroft enterprise, Henry Oak, to tell the news.[21] The originals in Washington finally and fully confirmed what they all had thought, i.e., that the documents in Bancroft's possession were not only true and accurate, but all that there was on the subject. Frémont was now doubly damned: not only was Larkin surely the only agent and the policy of peace towards the *Californios* the government's only policy, there were no instructions to Fremont at all. Even so, Royce was a cautious scholar, and wanted to give the Frémont's another chance to exonerate themselves.

In the summer of 1885, Royce made another visit to the Frémont's. He later reported to Henry Oak in Berkeley what had transpired. Royce pleaded with the Frémont's for something new from them that would shed a different light on "The Bear Flag Affair" now that the government's secrets were out. The conversation was cordial, Royce wrote, with the General "dignified and charming," and Mrs. Frémont "calm, sunny and benevolent." But, in the face of the facts, Royce told Oak, Frémont "lied, lied unmistakably, unmitigatedly, hopelessly. And that was his only defence[sic]."[22]

---

20. Andrew Rolle, *John Charles Fremont: Character as Destiny* (Norman: University of Oklahoma Press, 1991) 260.

21. Letter, Royce to Scudder, April 14, 1885, Scudder papers, Berkeley; Letter, Royce to Oak, April 14, 1885, Oak papers, Berkeley.

22. Letter, Royce to Oak, August 8, 1885, Oak papers, Berkeley.

As we end our specific interest in John C. Frémont, we must ask why Royce was so agitated, even angry, about what he called "Frémont's league with the devil." Kevin Starr suggests that Royce's anger turned on his belief that Frémont had committed what Starr calls "the original sin of California history." That sin turned on violating America's stated policy of bringing a Spanish-speaking society already in California into statehood with dignity and respect, not violence. Instead, as Starr writes, "the gallant captain had baptized California in blood, and Royce wanted historians of the state to face up honestly [to] that horrible burden."[23]

Royce's *California*, published in 1886, caused a strong reaction among those interested and involved in the early history of California and in the reputations made in those years. Royce seemed to be aware of what he had done. In a letter to a friend he wrote: "My book is full of kindling that I split and matches that I collected to heat the water . . . let the water boil."[24]

However, Royce was surprised by the virulence of the attacks on him and his book, and the friendships it would cost him; he was equally surprised at the lengths he would have to go to defend what he had written. It baffled Royce that his history was not being taken seriously by the California elite. Many ignored it and when they discussed it at all that tried to dismiss it saying, in effect, that the book was a version of the East coast patronizing one might expect from someone at Harvard. There was little appetite among leaders in California at that time to wrestle with Royce's main contention: that California in fact did succeed in creating a good community, but only after it dealt with its violent and racist past. They were largely in denial about the racism of the early years, and they didn't want to hear about from one of their native sons, especially if he was back East now.[25]

We now take a few pages to summarize the actual contents of the book. But, enough for now to say that Josiah Royce's venture into the waters of California history was far stormier that he had imagined it would be. It is not so much that he was "naive," as one historian charged[26] but that the issues he raised were—and are—troublesome to those who care about California history. Royce's book allows us to begin to see an alternate narrative for the early history of California.

23. Starr, *California Dream*, 159.
24. Quoted in ibid., 163.
25. Ibid., 164.
26. Rolle, *Fremont*, 260.

A Brief Summary of *California*

Royce's *California* revealed his independent mind. Of himself he said, "Because I am a Californian [I am] little bound to follow mere tradition."[27] In fact, his rendition of early California history flew in the face of a traditional American, i.e., "manifest destiny," viewpoint. Royce wanted his history to be more that merely a factual recounting of early days; he was interested in the events of history for themselves but even more so for "their value as illustrating American life and character."[28] That paradoxical "character" was displayed, as Royce saw it, on the one hand as careless, hasty and blind to social duties; on the other hand as "cheerful, energetic, courageous and teachable" (2).

Royce does not really doubt the inevitability of the eventual American conquest, nor, in his view, did the *Californios*. What the latter feared was the coming of bad Americans. The good American, to Mexicans and to Royce, is represented by Thomas Larkin, who was "the only American official who can receive nearly unmixed praise" for his work in California (38). The bad American is, represented by John C. Frémont. For Royce, history was not to be a happy patriotic story. Rather, he wrote the book "to serve the true patriot's interest in a clear self-knowledge and in the formation of sensible ideals of national greatness" (49). *California*, therefore, is the true parent of Limerick's *Legacy of Conquest*, for in it Royce sees that "conquest" is indeed the right word (not just "movin' west"), and that the attitudes of conquest continued after 1846. Those attitudes, Royce insisted, which the American "national character made us assume towards the Californians at the moment of our appearance among them as conquerors, we have ever since kept, with disaster to them, and not without disgrace and degradation to ourselves" (49).

Royce is particularly hard on the leaders of "The Bear Flag" uprising, especially Robert Semple, William B. Ide and of course Frémont. Royce mounts the evidence against them and finds their actions wanting in moral character; at one point saying they amounted to "atrocity" (135). Further, the very basis of the state reveals this uneasy conscience about the conquest, Royce insists. The lines most quoted by scholars and journalists from *California* are these: "The American as conqueror is unwilling to appear in

---

27. *Fugitive Essays* (Cambridge, MA: Harvard University Press. 1920) 7.
28. *California*, vii. Hereinafter all references to the book will appear parenthetically in the text, with the pages listed referring to the original 1886 edition.

public as a pure aggressor... The American wants to persuade not only the world, but himself, that he is doing God service in a peaceable spirit, even when he violently takes what he has determined to get" (151). While Royce would have no part in such hypocrisy, he would not judge all Californians. He rather preferred noting the irony that while the Mexican War had come to be regarded with "shame and contempt," the acquisition of California continued to be regarded as "a God-fearing act... [and part of] our devotion to the cause of freedom" (156). In this respect, Royce hoped his book would be a reminder and a guide for the future:

> So that when our nation is another time about to serve the devil, it will do so with more frankness, and will deceive itself less by half-conscious cant. For the rest, our mission in the cause of liberty is to be accomplished through a steadfast devotion to the cultivation of our own inner life, and not by going abroad as missionaries, as conquerors, or as marauders among weaker peoples. (156)

The singular injustice perpetrated by Frémont and Commander Sloat was the second conquest of the *Californios* in 1847, thereby sealing an ineradicable division between Anglo and Mexican Californians. When the *Californios* resented, sometimes resisted this, they came to be seen by Americans as rebels and traitors, which, Royce thought, forged "one more link in the fatal chain of injustice" (194).

The Gold Rush is portrayed within Royce's overall thesis of order and disorder. With thousands of new settlers arriving in 1849-50, the new state was subjected to further scenes of racism and anti-foreign feeling. Drawing from his own family's difficult trek to California in 1849, Royce noted the "religious" aura often associated with arrival in California, and the consequent attitude of high expectations among the new settlers. They hoped for, even expected, a great deal, so that when "foreigners" got in their way there was often violent reaction. Royce regards such actions as a "disgrace" to American ideals of liberty and fairness. So-called "miner's justice" was more than disgraceful, it retarded social maturity in the Anglo-American community by instilling a kind of thinking that quick, unambiguous justice could be had cheaply. Royce's passion shows clearly when he described the easy operation of lynching juries in convicting a "greaser" on little evidence: "One could see his guilt, so plainly, we know, in his ugly, swarthy face, before the trial began ... And if he was a native California, a born "greaser," then so much the worse for him" (363-64). Yet despite the passion, or perhaps because of it, Royce marvels at the way in which mining communities could learn from this "inner social disease" and begin the process of renewal within a generation. They were, in the end, able to found real communities, that is, in his terms, to move "from social foolishness to social steadfastness" (375).

In Royce's discussion of San Francisco's first ten years, we find "dramatic incidents that belong to the painful side of the struggle for order" (378). He contradicts thoroughly an early version of pioneer mythology that reveled in the "wicked" history of the city. To the contrary, the legend of gambling men and easy women were "but the froth on the turbid current" (398). The transient quality of early San Francisco life did indeed leave the stain of individuality that forsook social duty. But that was overcome by institutions of a conservative character, especially churches and families that showed people their social duty. The committees of vigilance were, of course, of great concern to the early history of San Francisco, and once again Royce goes right to the heart of the matter. In the famous case of the murder of the reform-minded editor, James King of William, by James Casey, Royce was the first scholar to see the significance of the social composition of the vigilance committee. In seems that "the best men" of San Francisco thwarted mob rule by asserting its own social and economic power. It was, as Royce noted, "A businessman's revolution" (440).

Royce's final subject is the emotionally-charged dispute over land titles. He wanted respect for the guarantees given the *Californios* at the time of the conquest. Most of the guaranteed land titles were not honored because of what Royce called "the rapacity" of "predatory disregard" by the Americans (467). The Land Act of 1851, according to Royce, only slightly dignified the wholesale movement of land from Californian to American hands. Worse yet, for Royce, was that the land manipulated away from the *Californios* did not end up in the hands of ordinary Americans, but in the greedy hands of speculators and lawyers. This was, he says, to cause "lasting injury" to the whole state of California.

In conclusion, Royce re-states that California history is more than a local or regional concern. In his view, California in the 1850s was an immature society characterized by social irresponsibility; by people who "love mere fullness of life and lack reverence for the relations of life" (500). Finally, the community did find a kind of social "salvation," but only because it learned the lessons it had heretofore "despised and forgotten." For Royce, it was only by Californians "confessing" that past to each other that the way forward could be found.

Royce's *California* and "The New Western History"

There has been a sea-change in the way we think about American history. It has happened in the past generation, and its consequences are still shaking American academic life. We should look into the new way of doing history to see how Royce's insights have continuing salience.

Among the vast literature about historical study there is one recent book that is singularly useful in demonstrating the ways in which history has changed. It is *Telling the Truth About History*, by Joyce Appleby, Lynn Hunt and Margaret Jacob.[29] By "telling the truth" Appleby and her colleagues do not mean to imply that other, prior historians were telling "lies." Rather, they mean that there was once a single narrative about American history that most Americans (African Americans, Native Americans, Latinos and women excepted) accepted as part of their heritage. It was a story of achievement, of how a nation of immigrants made the first liberal democracy, and how that nation became the economic success story of modern world history.

When historians extend the scope of American history beyond dominant groups the historical picture changes. Moreover, there is a new emphasis on the "standpoint" of the historian her/himself. Just as acknowledging the social location of historical subjects is important in getting a more fully-orbed picture of reality, so is the intellectual location of the historian important in terms of the questions asked and the answers sought. As the Appleby team [importantly three women], writes, "We routinely, even angrily, ask: whose history? Whose science? Whose interests are being served by these ideas and stories? The challenge is out to all claims of universality."[30]

This idea—what we call "the social construction of knowledge"— has transformed how we think about the history of the American West. American history, in its academic, professional setting, grew up with the history of the West. In a path-breaking essay in 1893, "The Significance of the Frontier in American History,"[31] Frederick Jackson Turner articulated a vision for American history that has been hard to shake. While many

---

29. *Telling the Truth about History* (New York: Norton, 1997).

30. Ibid., 9.

31. This famous essay is most conveniently found as the first chapter in Turner's *The Frontier in American History* (New York: Holt, 1920).

important points can be adduced from Turner, two are vital: that American interaction with the frontier provided an essential way of understanding the development of democracy in America; that the frontier "closed" about 1890, thus ending forever the most "American" phase of American history.

Several generations of historians have reacted to Turner in a variety of ways. But most importantly for our purposes, the newer versions of western history ask different questions than did Turner and his followers. Today we want to know the experience of women, natives and other "outsiders" because we want to know a total history of the West, not just "how the West was won." Moreover, the practitioners of this newer mode of historical discourse question the whole notion of "conquest" in moral terms. Instead of how the West was "won," we look at the historic treatment of natives, non-whites, women and even the land itself, and we might ask how the West was abused, oppressed, and, some might even say, "raped." This, in short, is a discussion of a different order.

Larry McMurtry, the novelist, is worried that these new kinds of questions and histories "failure studies" of American Western history.[32] To be sure, the work of the various scholars of the newer style of doing Western history do indeed asked searching, even searing, questions about the triumphalist viewpoint that was taught in most American history texts until fairly recently. McMurty may be right to remind us that some of the uncomfortable truths coming out in the new Western history have long been known. But, he vitiates his own point, and unintentionally vindicates Limerick and others in noting that Americans typically have not wanted "to receive bad news from out West."[33] In the end, McMurty is doleful, asking "Are our myths safe for a few more years, or must we westerners face up to living with nothing more stirring that our suburbs now that John Wayne is dead?"[34] What is lost in the new story is not the real American West; that was always, as Woody Guthrie observed, "hard, ain't it hard" for the people and the land.

For McMurtry and others what is lost is the West of the imagination. He reports having once noted sadness in his aged father's eyes, a sadness begotten of having known the newness of the West and now to know that his children would never see it. While one does not belittle McMurtry's

---

32. Larry McMurtry, "How the West Was Won or Lost," *The New Republic* (1999) 32–38.

33. Ibid., 33.

34. Ibid., 32.

wounded memory, the historians of the newer mode also see sadness in aged eyes; but those of the native people on marginal reservations and of the migrant workers picking fruits and vegetables in the Imperial Valley. The "conquest" was also about them and their ancestors, and Patricia Nelson Limerick is right to call our attention to the unbroken links between the past and the present.

The new western historians, especially Limerick, have been criticized from another direction, that they, especially she, have made too much of their own discovery of the tragic elements in western history. Especially forceful is the work of Forrest Robinson.[35] He notes Limerick's hope for a historian of the American West who could bring in the tragic element—as C. Vann Woodward had done for the South—and even suggests (some would say unfairly) that she ignored Royce in order to promote her own originality in that regard.[36]

The concerns of McMurtry and Robinson, to be fair, are important to scholars and students who would look anew at the history of California. As McMurtry himself writes, it is the West in our heads that we cannot let go of: "the very explorers who began the destruction of the Garden could not bear to admit that the Garden had been destroyed."[37] Robinson celebrates Royce for going against the temper of his own time and for displaying the courage to confront triumphalist ideologies. The issue for this historian is not faulting Limerick and others for forgetting Royce, but being glad that they remember him and his insights now; so that we all can face the future more realistically because we have acknowledged the past more courageously.

Moreover, to speak directly to McMurtry's lament, we agree that need not give up all the stories of the past even as we acknowledge the more recently discovered stories of other actors in the California drama. We need not give up the stories of hardship, bravery, courage and generosity now that we also know that there were, at least, equal measures of cowardice, treachery, greed and ill-gotten gain. Historian Richard Etulain has described with care and sensitivity the sorts of morally nuanced, socially complex and self-reflective stories that are needed for the new history to

---

35. Forrest G. Robinson, *The New Western History* (Tucson: University of Arizona Press, 1997).
36. Ibid., 80.
37. "How the West Was Won or Lost," 38.

unite past and future generations.[38] Patricia Limerick, in some of her recent writings, has written movingly about how the competing narratives might be reconciled, and the divisions "healed."[39]

Kevin Starr, whose multi-volume history of California has been previously mentioned, distinguishes himself once again, in an outstanding article, as California's preeminent historian. Even as he congratulates the recent historians for their new viewpoints, he asks that we not lose sight of what he calls "the founding time" of (American) California. In the context of the Gold Rush he concedes that it was not worth the cost of one Indian's child's life. He writes with both insight and deep feeling,

> Would it be better that the Gold Rush never happened? Is that what we are saying? Is that what were are saying when we contemplate the tragic dimensions of experience? Would it be better that there were no California? That we not be here? Which is to say that America not be here?[40]

Starr approvingly quotes Patricia Limerick, in her opening of the Gold Rush exhibit in Oakland, that human beings regularly do bad things. He invokes the Judeo-Christian tradition by calling these bad things "sins," which, when taken together "constitute a grave burden on the present because these sins are now a part of our living history."[41] Starr still wants to affirm the good and socially-useful aspects of early California history. But, for him, that affirmation must always be in tandem with an acknowledgement of "the sins of the fathers," and a determination "that these sins are not being recommitted in our own time." This is seen as California's "experiencing a prophetic probe, for better or for worse, of the larger American experience."[42]

As Robert Hine has suggested, Royce saw the history of the American West "as metaphysics," in which society moves from the willfulness of

---

38. "Western Stories for the Next Generation," *Western Historical Quarterly* 31 (2002) 5–23.

39. Patricia Nelson Limerick, Andrew Cowell, and Sharon K. Collinge, eds., *Remedies for a New West: Healing Landscapes, Histories and Cultures* (Tucson: University of Arizona Press, 2009).

40. Kevin Starr, "The Gold Rush and the California Dream," *California History* 77 (1998) 58.

41. Ibid., 61.

42. Ibid., 66.

individualism to the social cohesion of genuine community.[43] The glue that holds the community together, and at the same time prevents collectivist statism, is what Royce called "loyalty," a word probably better re-defined in our time as "solidarity." Some Roycean interpreters think this to be an essentially "religious" insight that has much to say about American values. Whether or not readers of *California* will agree with Royce will, of course, depend upon how that person constructs the moral life. But, Kevin Starr, the redoubtable critic who is conscious of "sin" in California's past presses us further: "And yet the moment we mention sin, we must also mention repentance, atonement, healing and forgiveness. . . .But for all the tangled burden of the past . . . [California] is struggling toward redemption and the light."[44]

Yet, despite Starr's impressive litany of "religious" actions, there is one missing: confession. It is precisely here that Royce's *California* is so compelling. Royce thought the early history of California to be of "divinely moral significance." He wrote his history for "any fellow Californian who may perchance note the faults of which I make confession."[45] He shows a way of social salvation, of solidarity within a community; for Royce that was the only saving grace. Whether or not Kevin Starr is right—that with "redemption" the "Pacific City on the Hill" can still flourish[46]—is for future generations of Californians to determine. Royce neither condemns nor condones all actions in early California history. He too seeks the balance that McMurtry, Starr and the latter Limerick, are looking for: of not emphasizing too much what Starr calls the dark side of California history and losing what McMurtry wants to retain, the West of the imagination.

Royce's *California*—a study of American character, as the subtitle proclaims—is the type of book that can help us to probe what Joan Didion called "the enigma" that is California,[47] It was not Royce's goal, nor should it be ours, to subvert one major narrative about the West in order to raise up another, but to disclose the multiple nature of realities in the West and California, and to probe the moral questions they pose.

---

43. Hine, *From Grass Valley to Harvard*, 166–85.
44. Starr, "The Gold Rush," 67.
45. Royce, *California*, 501.
46. Starr, "The Gold Rush," 67.
47. Joan Didion, *Where I Was From* (New York: Knopf, 2003).

"Let the Spirit Fly"

Marilynn Kramar and the History of the Latino/a Catholic Charismatic Movement in the U.S.-Mexico Borderlands

Gastón Espinosa

Introduction

"This goes out to all the homeboys listening. You know what? That's the real homeboy right there!" a twenty-something gang member said with tears streaming down his face one hot July evening in Los Angeles.[1] The "homeboy" was pointing to a picture of Jesus Christ vividly portrayed on a gigantic banner right behind him inside the Los Angeles sports arena. That night 15,000 Latinos/as from all over the United States and Latin America packed the sports arena to hear powerful testimonies and witness divine healing. No sooner had the "Vato Loco" finished his sentence than the stadium erupted with cheers and shouts of "gloria a Dios."[2] This "gang-member" had given his life to Jesus Christ. He claimed he was a new man. Standing next to him were about a dozen of other "homeboys" or gang members. After the shouts died down, a middle-aged, petite, blond-haired Euro-American woman, Marilynn Kramar, walked to center stage and hugged the stocky gang member. She then took the microphone and immediately began to lead the service in a time of enthusiastic singing, hand clapping, and worship. The energy radiating from the sports arena was electrifying. Between the testimonies, singing, and "praying in the spirit," Mexican Americans, Guatemalans, El Salvadorians, and Latinos

---

1. "Homeboy" is slang for a gang member.
2. "Vato Loco" is a Mexican-American gang expression for a "crazy dude."

from virtually every country in Latin America erupted in tongues, "singing in the spirit," and prayer. The ex-gang-member's testimony was only one part of this powerful, emotion-filled service.[3]

This was not a Benny Hinn or a Luis Palau miracle crusade, nor a Victory Outreach Church gang rally. Rather we witnessed a conference sponsored by Charisma in Missions, a Roman Catholic lay missionary evangelization society. Marilynn Kramar and Charisma in Missions have been two of the most important catalysts in the origins and development of the Latino/a Catholic Charismatic movement in the United States. She has helped unleash a potentially revolutionary movement that is transforming some dimensions of Latino/a popular Catholicism. According to Kramar, the organization has tens of thousands of people on their mailing lists and has touched the lives of an estimated three million Latino/a and Latin American Catholics throughout the U.S. and Latin America since it was organized in 1972. By almost any measure, she is one of the most important female Christian evangelists and renewal leaders of any tradition in the United States and Latin America in the late twentieth century.

Charisma in Missions has had its greatest impact in the Archdiocese of Los Angeles, where it has spawned hundreds of prayer groups in almost as many Catholic churches.[4] At first I disregarded many of the statistical claims made by Marilynn Kramar until a national survey found that more than twenty-six percent of all Latino/a Catholics identify as "born-again" Catholics, a term commonly used among Catholic charismatics. While not all "born-again" Catholics need be charismatic, it is, nonetheless, a term often used among this group of Catholics.[5] In 2014, a Pew Hispanic Survey reported that almost half of Latinos were charismatic, though I believe the 26 percent figure is more accurate because it is based on Catholic respondents affirming they were also both born-again and Pentecostal, Charismatic, or Spirit-filled, and not simply Charismatic, which is more

---

3. Charisma in Missions, promotional video (Montebello, CA: CharisMedia, n/d).

4. Charisma in Missions claims that its message has spread to over forty nations around the world. *Carisma en Misiones*, brochure (Montebello: *Carisma en Misiones*, n/d). Marilynn Kramar, interview by author, 15 October 1998, Montebello, California.

5. Gastón Espinosa, Virgilio Elizondo, and Jesse Miranda, *Hispanic Churches in American Public Life* (Notre Dame: Institute for Latino Studies at the University of Notre Dame, 2003) 1–17. The Pew Charitable Trust-funded national survey of Latinos, conducted in consultation with the Tomás Rivera Policy Institute in California, found that 26 percent considered themselves "born-again" Catholics and 22 percent said they affirmed they were Catholic, born-again, and Pentecostal/Charismatic, or Spirit-filled, all expressions very common and even encouraged by leaders in Charisma in Missions.

ambiguous.[6] If these numbers have been significantly shaped by Charisma in Missions, as I believe they have, its influence on Latino/a Catholicism may be much greater than scholars have hitherto realized.

Despite the growth of the Latino/a Catholic Charismatic movement, nothing has been written from a critical, scholarly perspective on it. This chapter will address this void in the historical literature by examining the origins and development of Charisma in Missions, the largest Latino/a Catholic Charismatic association in the United States. It will seek to answer a number of questions about this important yet overlooked renewal movement: What are its origins? What is its relationship to the larger Catholic Charismatic Renewal movement? What is its relationship to the Pentecostal movement? What problems does it face? Why has it grown so rapidly? What impact is it having on Latino/a Catholicism in the United States?

Origins of the Catholic Charismatic Renewal in the U.S.

Charisma in Missions does not trace its roots and impetus back to the Catholic Charismatic Renewal (CCR). Instead, Charisma in Missions traces its roots back to two former Anglo-American Assemblies of God missionaries to Colombia, Glenn and Marilynn Kramar. Despite this fact, Charisma in Missions has benefited greatly from the CCR because it cracked open the door for the Charismatic movement in the Catholic Church five years before the Kramars began their ministry in 1972.[7]

The larger Catholic Charismatic Renewal traces its roots back to two lay instructors in the department of theology at Duquesne University,

---

6. Pew Research Center, *The Shifting Religious Identity of Latinos in the United States*, chap. 7 (Washington, DC: Pew Hispanic Center Religion & Public Life, May 7, 2014) 1-2; Pew Research Center, *Changing Faiths: Latinos and the Transformation of American Religion*, April 25, 2007 (Washington, DC: Pew Research Center, Hispanic Trends, 2007) 1-3; http://www.pewhispanic.org/2007/04/25/changing-faiths-latinos-and-the-transformation-of-american-religion/.

7. Gastón Espinosa, "Catholic Charismatic Renewal," in Miguel De la Torre, ed., *Hispanic American Religious Cultures* (Santa Barbara, CA: ABC-CLIO, 2009) 1:95-98; Gastón Espinosa, "Kramar, Marilynn and Charisma in Missions," in Michael McClymond, ed., *Encyclopedia of Religious Revivals in America* (Westport, CT: Greenwood, 2007) 1:234-35; Gastón Espinosa, "Kramar, Marilynn" and "Charisma in Missions," in Stanley M. Burgess and Eduard M. Van Der Maas, eds., *The New International Dictionary of Pentecostal and Charismatic Movements* (Grand Rapids: Zondervan, 2002) 472-73 and 825-26.

Ralph Keifer and Patrick Bourgeois. In 1967, they became interested in the Pentecostal movement after reading David Wilkerson's *The Cross and the Switchblade* (1963) and John Sherrill's *They Speak with Other Tongues* (1964). Keifer became so curious about the Pentecostal movement that he began attending a Charismatic prayer group held in the home of a Presbyterian laywoman. A short while later, he received the baptism with the Holy Spirit. The mainline Protestant Charismatic movement thus served as an important bridge between the Pentecostal movement and the Roman Catholic Church.[8]

Keifer took his newfound experience back to Duquesne University, where he had his students read Wilkerson and Sherrill in his theology classes. In February, Keifer and Bourgeois organized a weeklong prayer meeting in which they encouraged their students to reflect on the first four chapters of the book of Acts. Over the weekend, a number of Catholic students received the baptism of the Holy Spirit. Shortly thereafter, Keifer, Bourgeois, and their students organized the first Catholic Charismatic prayer group at Duquesne University. This series of events helped birth the Catholic Charismatic Renewal movement in the United States.[9]

From its origins in Pittsburgh, the Catholic Charismatic Renewal spread very rapidly throughout the United States, especially to the University of Notre Dame. Ralph Martin and Stephen Cook, two recent graduates of Notre Dame, quickly became leaders of the fledgling movement. By late 1967, the movement was attracting the attention of major national Catholic weeklies such as *The National Catholic Reporter* and *Our Sunday Visitor*.[10]

The first nationwide Catholic Charismatic convention took place at Notre Dame on April 7–9, 1967. By the early 1970s, the Catholic Charismatic movement attracted the support of national and international Catholic leaders like Father Kilian McDonnell and the Belgian Cardinal, Leon Joseph Suenens. The movement grew rapidly throughout the 1970s,

---

8. T. P. Thigpen, "Catholic Charismatic Renewal," in Stanley M. Burgess and Eduard M. Van Der Maas, eds., *The New International Dictionary of Pentecostal and Charismatic Movements* (Grand Rapids: Zondervan, 2002) 460–67; F. A. Sullivan, "Catholic Charismatic Renewal," in Stanley M. Burgess and Gary B. McGee, eds., *Dictionary of Pentecostal and Charismatic Movements* (Grand Rapids: Zondervan, 1992) 111–12; Vinson Synan, *The Twentieth-Century Pentecostal Explosion: The Exciting Growth of Pentecostal Churches and Charismatic Renewal Movements* (Altamonte Springs, FL: Creation House, 1980) 39–53.

9. Sullivan, "Catholic Charismatic Renewal," 111–12.

10. Ibid., 112–14; Edward D. O'Connor, *The Pentecostal Movement in the Catholic Church* (Notre Dame: Ave Maria, 1971) 39–107.

attracting over 30,000 participants to its national conference at Notre Dame in 1976. By 1986, the movement claimed an estimated 6,000 prayer groups throughout the United States. The enormous enthusiasm and energy produced by the new movement quickly spread to Bolivia in 1969, Mexico and Peru in 1970, and Puerto Rico in 1971. Andrew Chesnut has noted that millions of "predominantly poor" Latin Americans have left Catholicism to join the Pentecostal movement and millions of other Catholics have become Charismatic. Unlike previous popes, who viewed the Charismatic movement with suspicion, Pope Francis has been supportive.[11] In the United States alone, the movement has grown from thirty students and two professors in 1967 to an estimated 12 percent of all U.S. Catholics in 2017, who make up approximately 23 percent of all Americans (325 million). Today, the varying types of the Catholic Charismatic renewal exist in over 230 countries, with an estimated 160 million participants.[12]

---

11. R. Andrew Chesnut, "The 50th Anniversary of the Greatest Movement Few Have Heard of," *Religion News Service* (February 20, 2017) 1–5; Pew Research Center, *Religion in Latin America: Widespread Change in a Historically Catholic Region* (Washington, DC: Pew Research Center Religion & Public Life, November 13, 2014) 1–5.

12. David Masci, "Why Has Pentecostalism Grown So Dramatically in Latin America?" (Washington, DC: Pew Research Center, November 14, 2014) 1–10; Gastón Espinosa, "The Pentecostalization of Latin American and U.S. Latino Christianity," *Pneuma: The Journal for the Society of Pentecostal Studies* 26, no. 2 (2004) 262–92; O'Connor, *Pentecostal Movement in the Catholic Church*, 39–107; Sullivan, "Catholic Charismatic Renewal," 112–15; Synan, *The Twentieth-Century Pentecostal Explosion*, 39–53; Patrick Johnstone, *Operation World* (Grand Rapids: Zondervan, 1993) 21–23; John Jessup, "Pope Francis Makes Overtures to Charismatic Catholics," *CBN News*, September 27, 2015, http://www1.cbn.com/cbnnews/us/2015/September/Pope-Francis-Makes-Overtures-to-Charismatic-Catholics; Cindy Wooden, "Pope Plans Pentecost Celebrations with Charismatics and Pentecostals," *Catholic News Service*, May 2, 2017, https://www.ncronline.org/news/vatican/pope-plans-pentecost-celebrations-charismatics-and-pentecostals. For more on the Catholic Charismatic movement in Latin America, see Edward L. Cleary, *The Rise of Charismatic Catholicism in Latin America* (Gainesville: University Press of Florida, 2011). For more about the CCR and its fifty-year Jubilee, see http://www.nsc-chariscenter.org/; and http://www.nsc-chariscenter.org/wp-content/uploads/2016/10/Revised-Final-Jubilee-Statement-1.pdf. For more about the size and scope of the Catholic Charismatic renewal around the world, see Alessandra Nucci, "The Charismatic Renewal and the Catholic Church," *The Catholic World Report*, May 18, 2013, http://www.catholicworldreport.com/2013/05/18/the-charismatic-renewal-and-the-catholic-church/; Molly Worthen, "Charismatic Catholicism Is Alive and Well," *CRUX: Taking the Catholic Pulse*, September 26, 2014, https://cruxnow.com/faith/2014/09/26/charismatic-catholicism-is-alive-and-well/.

Pentecostals on the Road to Rome

Unlike the CCR, which traces its roots back to mainline Protestant charismatics, Charisma in Missions traces its origins directly to the Pentecostal movement in the United States. Two Anglo-American Assemblies of God Pentecostal missionaries to Colombia, Glenn and Marilynn Kramar, founded Charisma in Missions in Los Angeles in the winter of 1972. Their decision to found Charisma in Missions and shortly thereafter join the Roman Catholic Church was shaped by their experience in Colombia.

Marilynn Roberts was born on May 5, 1939, to Bill and Lorine Roberts, and grew up an only child in the home of an Assemblies of God minister. The supernatural has always been a profound interest to Marilynn, who believes she was miraculously healed of a tumor at three months of age. Marilynn had a deep admiration both for her father and for an Assemblies of God missionary named Gladys Pearson. The latter was an excellent preacher who inspired Marilynn to consider becoming an evangelist or missionary. At age fifteen, Marilynn felt called to go into the evangelistic ministry. At age eighteen, in 1957, she married Earl Glenn Kramar, and together they conducted evangelistic and social work with the homeless and disadvantaged in Los Angeles. Shortly thereafter, they moved to Springfield, Missouri, where Glenn studied at Central Bible Institute (CBI) of the Assemblies of God. He earned a Bachelor of Arts degree in Bible in 1961. Marilynn did not attend CBI, but instead worked as a secretary. After the Kramars ministered in northern California a short while, Gladys Pearson persuaded the Kramars to go overseas as missionaries. They took up her challenge and, after receiving Assemblies of God approval and one year of language study in Guadalajara, Mexico, arrived in Colombia in March of 1966. Assemblies of God leaders in Bogotá quickly recognized Glenn's administrative abilities. In the summer of 1966, Glenn was elected superintendent of the entire Assemblies of God work in Colombia, made up of approximately 250 churches and missions. Glenn's task was made much easier by the assistance of his wife, Marilynn, and a Colombian named Esther Garzón. The work in Colombia blossomed under Glenn Kramar's administration.[13]

---

13. Gastón Espinosa, "Catholic Charismatic Renewal"; Gastón Espinosa, "Kramar, Marilynn and Charisma in Missions"; Gastón Espinosa, "Kramar, Marilynn" and "Charisma in Missions"; Marilynn Kramar and Robert C. Larson, *Joy Comes in the Morning: The Marilynn Kramar Story, The Birth of a Missionary Heart* (Ann Arbor, MI: Servant, 1990) 14–15, 22–24, 31. Additional information is taken from letters and two interviews

The Kramars became interested in Catholicism by accident. While they were working in Colombia, they heard reports of Catholic priests leading angry mobs against Assemblies of God pastors and parishioners out in the countryside. In one instance, Glenn drove out to a village where he and two other Colombian workers had their car vandalized and were almost stoned to death. This prompted Kramar, now the superintendent of the Assemblies of God in Colombia, to contact the nearest bishop and ask that he stop the persecution.[14]

To Kramar's surprise, the local Catholic bishop promised that he would put a stop to the attacks. He was also surprised a short while later to find that Archbishop Ocampo was conciliatory after Glenn protested the firebombing of Assemblies of God churches by fanatics. The more the Kramars began interacting with activist Catholic leaders like Father García Herreros, the more they became impressed by their openness, conciliatory attitude, spirituality, and desire to live out the recent promulgations of Vatican II. The Council not only called on Catholics to affirm what is true in Protestantism, but it also challenged Catholic leaders to reform the Church through evangelization, renewal efforts, and lay participation. All of this, along with the profound spirituality the Kramars noticed in the Catholic hierarchy, stood in stark contrast to the "Whore of Babylon" image they had grown up hearing about in the Pentecostal movement.[15]

The second major turning point in the Kramars' spiritual pilgrimage along the Road to Rome occurred when both Marilynn and Glenn had a vision in which they saw a Catholic priest holding up a chalice during a eucharistic service surrounded by hundreds of people enthusiastically "praising God."[16] They interpreted the vision as God leading them towards Roman Catholicism for some unknown reason. The next major turning point took place after they handed over the leadership of the Assemblies of God work in Colombia to native leaders and returned to Los Angeles in 1972. Although still affiliated with the Assemblies of God, they began to discuss Catholic theology with Father James O'Callaghan, pastor of St. John Vianney Catholic Church in Hacienda Heights. This jovial Irish priest spent

---

I conducted with Marilynn Kramar in the spring of 1997 and fall of 1998. Marilynn Kramar, Telephone interview by the author, April 1997, Hanover, New Hampshire; Marilynn Kramar, Interview by author, 15 October 1998, Montebello, California.

14. Kramar, *Joy Comes in the Morning*, 59–65.

15. Ibid., 59–65, 77–81, 103.

16. Ibid., 66.

the next few months answering the Kramar's questions about the Catholic faith. Shortly thereafter, they attended a Catholic Charismatic Renewal service where they heard Bishop Joseph McKinney preach about the Catholic Charismatic movement in the United States. More importantly, McKinney showed a film about the CCR in which they saw a chalice—like the one they had seen in their vision. They interpreted this accident of history as a providential event and a sign that God was leading them in the direction of the Roman Catholicism.[17]

The next turning point in their spiritual pilgrimage toward Rome took place later that same year. Not long after they arrived in Los Angeles, the Kramars felt called to conduct outreach ministry to Latino/a Catholics in the United States. While still ministers in the Assemblies of God, they founded Charisma in Missions in the summer of 1972. Shortly after the Kramar's began Charisma in Missions, the General Secretary of the Foreign Missions Boards of the Assemblies of God, Melvin Hodges, began receiving complaints that the Kramars were identifying too much with the Catholic Church. One person wrote, "Several [Assemblies of God workers] have come to the conclusion that the Assemblies of God is sponsoring missionary work in the Catholic Church to build it up" and that they have "gone too far in trying to identify with the Catholics." Still others were upset by Glenn's claim that "Catholics . . . [were] part of the body of Christ."[18] Rumors began to circulate that Glenn was wearing a Catholic collar, that Marilynn prayed the rosary and said "Hail Mary's," and that they were too close to the Catholic hierarchy in Colombia during their missionary tours in the summer of 1972 and winter of 1973.[19]

Hodges wrote a sharp letter to the Kramars warning them not to become too close to the Catholic Church because it was "not part of the True Church." The Kramars wrote back that the allegations against them were unfounded. Their only desire was to see "genuine spiritual reformation within the Roman Catholic Church." Although the Kramars admitted that they were going through a spiritual "identity crisis," they hoped the

---

17. Ibid., 88–93.

18. Floyd Woodworth, Letter to Melvin Hodges, 12 October 1972, Los Angeles, California.

19. Glenn Kramar, Letter to Melvin Hodges, 11 October 1972, Los Angeles, California; Glenn Kramar, Letter to Melvin Hodges, 27 October 1972, Los Angeles, California; Marilynn Kramar, "A Short Resume of Our First Three Weeks of Ministry in Latin America Beginning August 21, 1972, Los Angeles, California"; Marilynn Kramar, "Our Second Trip into Latin America, 10 January–14 February 1973, Los Angeles, California."

Assemblies of God would continue to sponsor their work financially in the Catholic Church.[20]

Their hope did not materialize. The decisive turning point in their spiritual journeys came in the winter of 1972. In December, Father O'Callaghan arranged a dinner meeting between the Kramars and Cardinal Timothy Manning of the Archdiocese of Los Angeles. Having just attended a *Cursillo*, Cardinal Manning was very interested in the Kramars' desire to start a lay renewal ministry among Latino/a Catholics in the Archdiocese.[21] After an extended dialogue, the Cardinal offered his blessing for the formation of a non-profit society aimed at spiritual renewal and evangelization. When the Kramars asked Cardinal Manning how they should proceed, he responded by stating that they should, "Let the bird [Holy Spirit] fly. Let the Lord show you what to do next." This statement became the turning point in the Kramars' decision to join the Roman Catholic Church. Marilynn wrote: "Out of that night came the conviction that God not only was calling us to the Catholic Church, but giving us a commission as well."[22]

In January 1972, the Kramars asked the Assemblies of God to become joint sponsors with the Catholic Church of their Charisma in Missions ministry. They not only had the support of Archbishop Manning, but also Father James O'Callaghan, now on the board of directors of Charisma in Missions. Rank-and-file members of the Assemblies of God questioned the Kramars' judgment and loyalty. The Division of Foreign Missions committee summoned the Kramars to Springfield to find out where their ultimate commitment lay. After a friendly conversation, they mutually decided that the Kramars should voluntarily withdraw their affiliation from the Assemblies of God and hand in their ministerial credentials. Now that their affiliation with the Assemblies of God was severed, they decided to join the Roman Catholic Church. They were officially received into the Catholic

---

20. Melvin Hodges, Letter to Glenn Kramar, 5 October 1972, Springfield, Missouri; Glenn Kramar, Letter to Melvin Hodges, 27 October 1972, Los Angeles, California; Glenn and Marilynn Kramar, Letter to Rev. Barlette Peterson, 20 March 1973.

21. The Cursillo is an intense weekend experience of spiritual renewal. Spanish airforce pilots training at an air base in Texas first brought it over to the U.S. from Spain in 1947. The movement was and still is very popular in the Catholic Church. By 1976, about 300,000 people had made a *Cursillo*, including fifty to sixty bishops and almost 7,000 nuns and priests. Moises Sandoval, *On the Move: A History of the Hispanic Church in the United States* (Maryknoll, NY: Orbis, 1990) 84–85.

22. Kramar, *Joy Comes in the Morning*, 83–103.

Church through "conditional baptism" on May 29, 1973. Their spiritual journey along the road to Rome had come to its conclusion.[23]

Birth of Charisma in Missions

The one-time Assemblies to God-financed ministry was now transformed into a lay Catholic ministry blessed by the Archdiocese of Los Angeles. For this reason, Charisma in Missions marks the birth of the organization from the month they received the pastoral blessing by Cardinal Manning in December 1972. The purpose of Charisma in Missions is to promote evangelism, conversion, spiritual renewal, and spiritual and social welfare programs in the Latino/a Catholic community in the United States and Latin America. It sponsors a number of programs and events like the International Latin Encounter, the Latin Encounter for Youth, the Annual Married Couples Convention, the Catholic Campaign of Faith, *Presencia*—One-Day Faith Rallies, the Missionary Institute of Proclaimers, Good News Courses, Children's Ministry, Drama Ministry, and most importantly, Growth Seminars. To support these ministries it has developed a number of departments such as CharisBooks, CharisTapes, CharisMedia, and CharisPublications. Their goal is to bring about "spiritual renewal" and "reformation" within the Catholic Church. Kramar said that the Bible and Vatican II "outlined our mission in the church—to rattle new life into dry bones within the household of God . . . Our job was to evangelize baptized Catholics who either didn't fully understand or were not actively involved in the life of faith."[24]

---

23. Glenn and Marilynn Kramer, Letter to Rev. Barlette Peterson, 20 March 1973; Glenn and Marilynn Kramar, Circular Fundraising Letter, 4 April 1973, Los Angeles, California; Glenn Kramar, Letter to Don Stuckless, 8 May 1973, Los Angeles, California.

24. For more about Charisma in Missions and Kramar, see Charisma in Missions website: http://www.carismaenmisiones.org/; Gastón Espinosa, "Catholic Charismatic Renewal"; Gastón Espinosa, "Kramar, Marilynn and Charisma in Missions"; Gastón Espinosa, "Kramar, Marilynn" and "Charisma in Missions"; Kramar wrote, "I find great comfort in the promises from the documents of Vatican II. In the 'Dogmatic Constitution on the Church,' the council fathers speak of the mystery of the church saying, 'The Holy Spirit guides the Church into the fullness of all truth and gives her a unity of fellowship and service. He furnishes and directs her with various gifts both hierarchical and charismatic' (ch. 1, no. 4)." Marilynn Kramar, *Charisma in Missions: Catholic Missionary Evangelization Society* (Montebello, CA: Charisma in Missions, ca. 1990s). Kramar, *Joy Comes in the Morning*, 100, 144.

All of these factors have contributed to Charisma in Missions' tremendous growth since 1972. In 1975, Charisma in Missions, with the support and blessing of Bishop Juan Arzube, began holding The International Latin Encounter for Renewal & Evangelization, better known as the Latin Encounter (*Encuentro Latino*). The annual Latin Encounter has grown in attendance from 600 participants in 1975 to 20,000 participants from twenty-five countries in 2017. Charisma in Missions-initiated prayer groups in the Archdiocese of Los Angeles have increased in number from one in 1975, to 140 in 1983, and hundreds by 2017.[25]

Charisma in Missions has witnessed such tremendous growth over the years that it purchased land in East Los Angeles and built the *Porciuncula* or Catholic Center for Evangelization. The modestly furnished center is now the highly-successful international headquarters of Charisma in Missions. It was named and dedicated by Cardinal Timothy Manning on December 10, 1982. Named after the "small portion" (*porciuncula*) of land given to St. Francis of Assisi, the *Porciuncula* center consists of two large buildings, twenty-four classrooms, two kitchens, two large conference rooms, a large gymnasium (seating 1,000) people, a print shop, a mail room, a bookstore, and tape and media departments. Its facilities are the sacred center and hub of Charisma in Missions in the United States and one of the key launching points for the Charismatic movement in Latin America. Although the *Porciuncula* is not a church, it sponsors weekly and monthly programs such as The Rosary in the Family, a weekly Healing Mass, Family Healing, Leadership Day, Nights of Growth, and Nights of Praise. Twenty full-time employees that serve about 2,000 people a week and hundreds of thousands of people a year throughout the U.S. and Latin America staff the *Porciuncula* complex.[26]

Charisma in Missions is based in Los Angeles, but its ministry reverberates throughout the United States and forty nations throughout Latin America and around the world. It sponsors a number of radio ministries and the weekly television program ¡Alabare! (I Will Praise Him). This program is aired through cable throughout the U.S. and Latin America. In addition to their television and radio programs, Charisma in Missions also

---

25. Charisma en Misiones, "Encuentro Latino Internacional de Los Angeles," http://www.carismaenmisiones.org/encuentro-latino-internacional-de-los-angeles.html. Kramar, *Charisma in Missions*, 25. Delia Almaraz, Telephone interview by the author, 5 October 1998, Santa Barbara, California. Kramar, *Joy Comes in the Morning*, 108–10.

26. Marcia Ford, "Pentecostal Missionary Now Directs Catholic Ministry," *Charisma* (1995) 25. Kramar, *Joy Comes in the Morning*, 97–99.

produces its own music tapes and books for sale throughout the U.S. and Latin America.[27] Kramar serves as Vice-President and General Manager for two local commercial Spanish-language radio stations in Los Angeles.[28] Charisma in Missions claims that its ministries have touched the lives of tens of thousands of followers in the Archdiocese of Los Angeles alone and more than half a million Latinos/as every year across the U.S.[29]

Theology of the Latino/a Catholic Charismatic Movement

Charisma in Missions, with its roots back to the Pentecostal-Charismatic movement has adapted its Pentecostal message to the Catholic Church. It has blended Pentecostal and Catholic spirituality to create a new hybrid tradition that appeals to both traditional Catholics and those seeking a more experiential faith. This is evident in the Charismatic Mass. Although the Eucharist is the central event of the Mass, prayer, praise, testimony, and short homilies or sermons also surround it. In many services prayer group leaders set aside time to pray for the sick and divine healing. Latino/a Catholic charismatics, in contrast to their Latino/a Protestant Pentecostal counterparts, also have a warm appreciation and respect for tradition and popular piety. This respect for popular piety has its limits, however, as Mexican folk healing (*curanderismo*) is condemned in the strongest terms.[30]

In addition to making the Eucharist the central part of their services and respecting Church tradition, Latino/a Catholic charismatics also take a sacramental view of salvation and theology. Catholic dogma and teaching has affected their interpretation of tongues speaking. They reject the initial evidence theory of the baptism with the Holy Spirit—a position held by most classic Pentecostals. Instead, they distinguish between the sacramental baptism of the spirit whereby the gift of the Holy Spirit was actually conferred or imparted, and the Pentecostal baptism in the spirit, which is interpreted as a release of the power of the Holy Spirit in their lives. Thus in their interpretation, the spirit is already present in their lives but lies

---

27. Ford, "Pentecostal Missionary Now Directs Catholic Ministry," 22, 25.

28. Press Release, Marilynn Kramar Catholic Missionary Evangelist (Montebello, CA: Charisma in Missions, 1996), English-language press release.

29. Sandoval, *On the Move*, 104.

30. Marilynn Kramar, Interview by author, 15 October 1998, Montebello, California. Kramar, *Joy Comes in the Morning*, 135.

dormant. The spirit-baptism ignites an awareness of the gifts of the spirit already present in one's life.[31]

Latino/a Catholic charismatics also venerate the Virgin Mary and the saints, although some Charisma in Missions leaders like Delia Almaraz encourage Catholic charismatics to downplay the intermediary role of the saints in their prayer meetings and instead focus on Jesus Christ.[32] Although they do not emphasize the role of the saints, they do regularly display a picture or banner of Our Lady of Guadalupe in their services. The Brown Virgin is seen as an aid that leads people to Jesus Christ. Kramar likes to point out that Our Lady of Guadalupe is the patron saint of evangelization in Mexico. Speaking of the importance of Our Lady of Guadalupe, Kramar wrote: "To say we do not need Mary is to say to Jesus, 'I love you, but I don't want and I don't like your mom.' Mary is an instrument, the model of the Holy Spirit who leads us to her Son, Jesus." Although at most services hymns are sung to the risen Christ, normally at least one hymn is offered in honor Our Lady of Guadalupe.[33]

Impact of Charisma in Missions on Latino/a Catholicism

Charisma in Missions has had a notable impact on Latino/a Catholicism in the United States and Latin America. Next to the *Cursillo* movement, Charisma in Missions has been one of the most important vehicles for spiritual renewal and evangelization in Latino/a Catholicism. Thousands of disaffected Latinos/as have been ushered back into the Catholic Church because of Charisma in Missions. Speaking about the impact of Charisma in Missions at the annual Latin Encounter, Jorge Ortiz, a Salvadoran immigrant, stated, "The Catholic Church was asleep! The Church did not wake us up. Now it's alive. Right here! Right now!"[34] This newfound enthusiasm for the Church has helped to serve as a major bulwark against Latino/a Protestant

---

31. Kramar, *Joy Comes in the Morning*, 144–45.

32. Delia Almaraz first became involved with Charisma in Missions in 1974 at the San Gabriel Mission. It was there that she met Marilynn Kramar. She has worked for Charisma in Missions for approximately fifteen years as both a volunteer and paid employee. She also helped with the first Latin Encounter in 1975. Delia Almaraz, Telephone interview by the author, 5 October 1998, Santa Barbara, California.

33. Kramar, *Joy Comes in the Morning*, 146, 149–50. Margaret Ramírez, "Getting That Old-Time Religion," *Los Angeles Times*, 11 July 1999, B1, B6.

34. Kramar, *Joy Comes in the Morning*, 84–84, 134, 149.

and Pentecostal proselytism by offering Catholics many of the trappings of the Pentecostal movement without having to leave the Church.

Charisma in Missions has not only contributed to spiritual renewal and evangelization, it has also contributed to greater lay participation in the Catholic Church. Charisma in Missions has no paid clergy to lead the local prayer groups. With the exception of a few priests and sisters, lay people lead almost all of the prayer groups and large events. This is also true at the national level. While there are twenty people on staff at the *Porciuncula*, 1000 volunteers minister at hundreds of prayer group and evangelization meetings each year.[35] This heavy emphasis on lay participation and leadership has meant that thousands of Latinos/as are getting out of their pews and participating in the life of the Church. In a tradition where 88 percent of Latino/a Catholics are not very involved in the life of the Church, only 23 percent attend Mass regularly, and less than 5 percent of all priests are Latino, this movement is an important contribution to the local Church because it encourages lay participation and leadership.[36]

Charisma in Missions has also contributed to the rise of new Latino/a Catholic leadership. This is done indirectly by giving lay people an opportunity to serve their churches as prayer group leaders and directly through their school of evangelism. Charisma in Missions Institute of Proclaimers has trained hundreds of lay workers and more than fifty youth evangelists. It has also inspired many Latinos/as to go into the priesthood, Kramar said. The Institute not only prepares lay evangelists, but it also prepares lay leaders and teachers to organize and lead other ministries in their local churches. Furthermore, hundreds of Catholic priests have attended or participated at Charisma in Missions prayer groups and events since 1972.[37]

---

35. Ibid., 134.

36. Ibid. Gilbert Cadena, "Religious Ethnic Identity: A Socio-Religious Portrait of Latinas and Latinos in the Catholic Church," in *Old Masks, New Faces: Religion and Latino Identities*, edited by Anthony Stevens-Arroyo & Gilbert R. Cadena (New York: Bildner Center for Western Hemisphere Studies, 1994) 31–44. Roberto González and Michael LaVelle, *The Hispanic Catholic in the U.S.* (New York: Northeastern Pastoral Center, 1988), as cited in Kosmin and Lachman, *One Nation under God: Religion in Contemporary American Society* (New York: Harmony, 1993) 138–39. Luís Velásquez, Associate Director of Hispanic Ministry for the Archdiocese of Los Angeles, stated in the 1990s that probably no more than 20 percent of all Latino Catholics in his archdiocese attend Mass regularly. As cited in Russell Chandler, *Racing toward 2001: The Forces Shaping America's Religious Future* (San Francisco: HarperSan Francisco: 1992) 169–70.

37. Kramar, *Joy Comes in the Morning*, 134–35.

Perhaps not surprisingly, Charisma in Missions attracts a large number of women. Kramar's experience in Charisma in Missions changed her life and became a source of empowerment. Speaking about her growing ministry, she wrote, "I learned that Marilynn Kramar had a great deal more to offer the world than music and wifely advice. God had a special call on my life that was just now starting to come into focus." After her divorce she began to see that her success was not tied to her husband. Kramar wrote, "I began to discover . . . abilities I had which . . . had been suffocated or long forgotten . . . I awakened to the reality of my giftedness in administration as well as in preaching and teaching. Through the encouragement of friends and supporters, I began to see myself in a new light." Kramar has taken her experience and tried to serve as a role model for Latinas who are interested in organizing lay ministries in their local churches. While the prayer groups are technically under the leadership and authority of the parish priest, practically speaking it is usually women who organize, lead, and run the prayer groups, which are often the size of small congregations of 70 to 120 people. Women also play an equally visible and important role in the organization of Charisma in Missions. While men are disproportionately represented on the governing board, women do most of the work and reap most of the benefits of "hands-on ministry." Thus it is not surprising that women make up an estimated 65 percent of Latino/a Catholic charismatic participants.[38]

Charisma in Missions has made Los Angeles the sacred center and pilgrimage site for thousands of Latinos/as who pour into the city every year to attend the annual Latin Encounter. For the last ten years, pilgrims have traveled from 23 countries to Los Angeles to participate in the *Encuentro Latino*. In 2017, countless bus loads of pilgrims took the four-day bus ride from central Mexico to Los Angeles. This pilgrimage is likely to continue because while the Latin Encounter is taking place, Charisma in Missions also sponsors the Latin Youth Encounter. The event regularly attracts more than 5,000 youth, making it one of the largest annual Catholic youth events in North America.[39]

Charisma in Missions is contributing to the Pentecostalization of Latino/a Catholicism in the U.S. and Latin America. It has helped give birth to the Charismatic Mass. The roots of the Mass are located in Roman

---

38. Ibid., 102–3, 147.

39. Ford, "Pentecostal Missionary Now Directs Catholic Ministry," 25; Kramar, *Joy Comes in the Morning*, 11, 135.

Catholicism and the Pentecostal movement. Kramar is very open about the fact that she has taken the Pentecostal worship and evangelistic strategies she learned in the Assemblies of God and applied some of them to the Latino/a Catholicism. She wrote, "I will always treasure my background in the Assemblies of God. It helped me for my present work of evangelization. My ability to design programs, my life in the Spirit, my zeal to follow Christ, my enthusiasm for world missions, my desire to proclaim the Good News—all these gifts and abilities were developed . . . while I was still a child" in the Assemblies of God. She is also open about the influence of Billy Graham on her ministry. Kramar wrote, "We began to conduct rallies here in Los Angeles similar to the Billy Graham Evangelistic Campaign approach. I remember watching him once on television. People by the thousands streamed down to profess Jesus as Lord. I thought, 'My God, this message should be developed for a Catholic audience. We need to act upon our faith response and be reconciled and renewed. We need to live an authentic life of faith in the Lord." Kramar did precisely this. She organized Catholic evangelistic campaigns using lively music and testimony. She called for conversion and renewal. She reports that hundreds of thousands of people have answered her call as have thousands of other prayer group leaders across the U.S. over the past twenty-nine years.[40]

The results of these techniques have been notable. The influence of Charisma in Missions on U.S. Latino/a Catholicism is visible not only in the Charismatic Mass but also in increased lay participation and leadership in small group ministries, an emphasis on women in lay ministry, a greater ecumenical openness to Protestants and Pentecostals, an emphasis on a personal "born-again" relationship with Jesus Christ, and the rise of Charismatic consumer products such as the kind one might normally associate with Evangelical and Pentecostal Protestantism. At many Latino/a Catholic Charismatic prayer groups and events, one can find people wearing Christian T-shirts, singing Evangelical/Pentecostal camp songs, displaying Christian bumper stickers, and carrying thick Study Bibles with colorful Bible covers. Scattered on some tables, one can also find a few books and products written by Evangelical and Pentecostal writers.[41]

---

40. Kramar, *Joy Comes in the Morning*, 110, 132.

41. This became apparent to the author when he visited Charisma in Missions prayer groups, events, and the headquarters in Los Angeles. Ibid., 110–11.

"Bendita Crisis," Blessed Crisis: Conflicts in Charisma in Missions

The rapid growth of Charisma in Missions has come at a price, however. In 1978, the Kramar family was ripped apart by infidelity and divorce. Glenn, after spending two years in Rome to become a priest, became disillusioned by the process and with religion. After returning to Los Angeles in 1977, he had an affair with an ex-nun who was working at the Charisma in Missions headquarters. This affair went on for some time before Glenn asked Marilynn for a divorce. The affair shook Marilynn's faith and almost led to a breakdown for herself and her family. With her family falling apart around her, Marilynn turned to her extended family at Charisma in Missions and the Catholic hierarchy to put the pieces of her life back together again. In 1978, the Kramars divorced and Glenn married the other woman. Despite the tragedy of the divorce, Marilynn's work continued and prospered. In 1978 the Franciscan University of Steubenville, Ohio, granted her an Honorary Doctorate in Humanities for her many years of ministry among Latinos/as throughout the U.S. and Latin America.[42]

The dramatic crisis that Kramar went through almost led her to give up the Charisma in Missions ministry. The turmoil and confusion of her divorce led to a dramatic encounter with Cardinal Manning in which she laid the Charisma in Missions constitution, bylaws, accounting records, and literally the entire organization, at his feet. Marilynn stated to Cardinal Manning, "I can't do it alone. I have to have a covering. I can't do it by myself like this." She went on to write, "I was determined to give it over to the Lord by submitting it to my shepherd for his discernment and direction. It wasn't out of obligation. It was out of an earnest desire to be certain that God was in charge of my life. I needed and expected that reassurance." Cardinal Manning, shocked by Marilynn's display of helplessness, stated, "Girl, you can't quit. You have to promise me you'll keep going. Can't you see the grace of the Church falling on you now?"[43] Responding to her appeal for help, Cardinal Manning assigned Msgr. Donald Montrose to serve as her spiritual mentor and counselor. After this series of events, and a mar-

---

42. She has also served on the U.S. Catholic Bishop's Ad Hoc Committee for Evangelism, the Lausanne Committee of the Catholic Charismatic Renewal of the United States, and as a guest speaker for Women's Aglow Fellowship International. Press Release, *Marilynn Kramar: Fundadora de Carisma en Misiones Evangelizadora Católica* (Montebello, CA: Carisma en Misiones, January 1996); Kramar, *Joy Comes in the Morning*, 114–31.

43. Kramar, *Joy Comes in the Morning*, 144, 146.

riage annulment, Kramar began to put the pieces of her life back together again. Although she had already been directing Charisma in Missions for all practical purposes since Glenn left to go to Rome in 1975, she was now left as the primary leader of the movement. Kramar served as president of this movement until her death on April 3, 2017, after which time Esther Garzon stepped in to help lead the movement.

In addition to personal problems, Kramar and Charisma in Missions has also faced theological, institutional, structural, organizational, and financial difficulties. Despite the fact that the larger Catholic Charismatic Renewal movement had opened the doors of the Catholic Church to the Charismatic movement, there is still suspicion and lack of cooperation on the part of some Catholic priests and bishops. Regarding the opposition, Kramar stated, "If you have all of these Catholics jumping around, you can imagine what the priest is thinking. He doesn't know what to do with that. In the beginning [of the movement] a lot of charismatics acted like children, but children have to grow up." She went on to claim that people were attracted to the Charismatic movement because "this is religion that's exciting. It's upbeat. It's joyful. . . ."[44]

Charisma in Mission's emphasis on conversion, evangelism, missions, a "born-again" experience, speaking in tongues, enthusiastic worship services, and the spiritual gifts left it vulnerable to charges of introducing Protestantism into the Catholic Church. Catholic scholar Allen Figueroa-Deck stated, "Some of the criticism [against Charisma in Missions] comes out of discomfort with a style that is spontaneous and emotional and has roots in Pentecostalism. There is also a fear that this may be a prelude to moving out of the Catholic Church." In fact, Latinos/as are attracted to the movement because it gives people the opportunity to express themselves in a community that affirms spiritual, emotional and physical healing.[45]

Even within the Catholic Charismatic Renewal, Charisma in Missions is seen by some as being too Pentecostal and experience-oriented. Asking to remain anonymous, one leader in the CCR in Los Angeles stated that Charisma in Missions was "too emotional."[46] Kramar was well aware of these kinds of criticism and for this reason used to caution Catholic charismatics against excess. She also used to encourage people to read Fr. George De Prizio's, *Charismatic Follies,* to help them avoid extreme behavior. The

44. Ramírez, "Getting That Old-Time Religion," B6.
45. Deck as cited in ibid.
46. Ramírez, "Getting That Old-Time Religion," B6.

CCR's behind-the-scenes criticism is possibly driven by the fact that over the past decade it has witnessed a decline in numbers and participation at precisely the same time that Charisma in Missions has witnessed a notable increase. In an effort to stem the tide and fill this gap, for the first time several years ago the CCR began offering a large number of Spanish-language seminars at their annual conference. Although Kramar denied that she was bothered by CCR's decision to sponsor a large number of Spanish-language seminars aimed at Latino/a Catholics, one still wonders if she was simply withholding criticism to maintain peace.[47]

The Archdiocese of Los Angeles, other than giving its blessing in 1972, has done little to provide financial support for Charisma in Missions, until the mid-2000s. Largely, it has had to fend for itself and generate its own financial and volunteer lay support. This has actually helped to strengthen the organization and prayer groups because it has prompted Catholic laity to get involved in organizing, leading, and fundraising.

Despite Charisma in Missions' diligent work in the Latino/a community, it still faces a considerable level of indifference on the part of many Latino/a Catholics. While many are open to the movement, Charisma in Missions' direct emphasis on the "lordship of Christ" and a "spirit-filled relationship with God" has scared off some Latinos/as, according to Kramar before she died. However, although Charisma in Missions clearly makes Jesus Christ the center of its message and experience, and they also intentionally highlight Our Lady of Guadalupe and popular Catholic traditions. The long-term impact of Charisma in Missions on Latino/a popular religiosity is uncertain. For although many Latinos get involved with Charisma in Missions, many also leave the movement.

The most surprising opposition to Charisma in Missions has come from some Latino priests and lay leaders. Luís Velásquez, Director of Hispanic Ministry for the Archdiocese of Los Angeles, strongly admonished Charisma in Missions prayer group leaders and evangelizers for going through forty hours of training, or (as Kramar believed) "indoctrination." The purpose of the training is to raise the consciousness of Latino/a prayer group leaders and evangelizers and encourage them to participate in the political and social struggle of liberationist priests and activists on behalf of Latino/a Catholics. They want to make this training a requirement in order to be a prayer group leader. In a previous interview, she stated that

---

47. George De Prizio, *Charismatic Follies* (La Puente, CA: Charis, n/d); Marilynn Kramar, Interview by the author, 15 October 1998, Montebello, California.

some Latino priests and Hispanic offices are trying to control the movement and use it for their own political and social agenda. She opposed this because she believed it would destroy the movement's emphasis on spiritual renewal. In some respects, the prayer groups function organizationally like Christian Base Communities (CBCs) in Latin America. Although organizationally it seems that it would take very little effort to transform them into CBCs, in fact this would be very difficult to do because the ideological underpinnings of the two movements are very different in their theology, focus, and goals.[48]

Kramar's struggle with some liberationist priests and lay leaders was further complicated by the Los Angeles Archbishop assigning a liaison person who had never been involved in the CCR and was not in favor of the movement. At one point in her struggle, she received a letter from the Archdiocese informing her that "you are no longer the advisor" for the 250 charismatic prayer groups in Los Angeles. Some questioned her loyalty to the Catholic Church. Although Kramar did not believe that she was facing sexism or a glass ceiling, she did admit that they were "possibly trying to stop my freedom" and "take advantage of Hispanics to pursue 'Hispanic causes.'" She admitted that the present struggle was over "power and control" of Charisma in Missions and some aspects of the Charismatic movement. In a moment of frustration, Kramar stated that "some people would try do anything to suffocate the Holy Spirit's power. No one can control or duplicate the power of the Holy Spirit."[49]

Like any organization, Charisma in Missions has suffered from apostasy and drop out. Key leaders, especially men, have joined the organization only to drop out, and sometimes not on the best of terms. Whether or not this was due to Kramar's leadership style, a bias against women in ministry, burnout, or all of the above, is uncertain. One wonders whether Kramar would have been treated the way she has if she were an Anglo or Latino male layman, priest, or bishop.

The struggles over gender, ethnicity, and leadership are all intertwined. Much of the unspoken pressure from Latino priests often emerges because Kramar was not Latina and yet she had presided over an all-Latino/a organization for decades. This issue is further complicated by the fact that she had intentionally chosen not to identify, embrace, or propagate a Liberation

---

48. Marilynn Kramar, Interview by the author, 15 October 1998, Montebello, California.

49. Ibid.

Theology approach in her ministry. That approach is very common among Latino priests who are fighting against social, political, and ecclesiastical injustice in society and the Church. From a liberationist perspective, although Kramar had done a good job of mobilizing the masses, she had not given them the intellectual, social, and political tools to fight against injustice and bring about the Kingdom of God on earth. Thus, it is not surprising that some Latino priests would like to have seen her take a more liberationist and activist approach to ministry.

Explaining Growth

Why has Charisma in Missions grown so rapidly in the Latino/a community? Why do thousands of Latinos/as in the Archdiocese of Los Angeles and over 500,000 Latinos/as nationwide participate in Charisma in Missions initiated prayers groups and other events every year?

Charisma in Missions is growing for many of the same reasons that the larger Latino/a Pentecostal movement is growing. It places a heavy emphasis on evangelism and personal conversion. It offers Latino/a Catholics "new life in Jesus Christ" and a fresh start without having to leave the Catholic Church. Seventeen year-old Alejandra Ramírez described her experience in the Catholic Charismatic movement as a "stress reliever." She went on to say, "You deal with work and school and you come here and its like you're reborn. You feel like your body is here but your soul is somewhere else. You're really with God." In a similar vein, Salvadorian immigrant Miguel Morales said, "I was a dead man walking. Spiritually dead. Look at me now. All I want to do is praise God and thank him for what he's given me."[50]

Charisma in Missions also strongly encourages small group ministry and active lay participation in prayer groups and the local church. A leader of a prayer group does not have to be a priest or an educated person. In this respect, it provides an outlet, opportunity, and voice for lay leadership in the local church for an otherwise voiceless yet spiritually-minded people. It also affords women tremendous opportunities to evangelize, teach, and minister in their local parishes, albeit under the authority of the parish priest. For example, another woman, Esther J. Garzón, who had worked with Marilynn in Columbia, has been one of the primary teachers and

---

50. Ramírez and Morales as cited in Ramírez, "Getting That Old-Time Religion," B1, B6.

authors of the movement's training manuals, booklets, and resource guides. Women seem to find a certain level of worth and agency in Charisma in Missions and the CCR not found in other societies and organizations.[51]

The Latino/a Catholic Charismatic movement is also growing because it specifically targets families and youth. In a day when many Catholic Churches cannot afford to hire a youth director, the prayer groups often sponsor and/or provide the only leadership for many youth ministry programs and/or youth choirs. In this respect, the movement is reproducing itself and raising up a new generation of Latino/a Catholic charismatics in the Church. Another important reason why it is growing is that it is decentralized. The success or failure of a prayer group is completely dependent upon the will and commitment of the prayer group leaders and parishioners in each local church. In this respect, it creates internal lay leadership and more active parishioners. Finally, Charisma in Missions is growing because it is willing to use drama, contemporary music, and recreational events to attract and keep young people. Describing her experience at various Catholic charismatic events, Lydia Kahler said, "I get an uplifting feeling when I come here, kind of like a concert. It is like a giant pep rally for the Lord." Likewise, Noel Díaz stated, "It gives us an easier way to express our feelings, not only with our hearts, but with our hands, with our voice. More people are realizing they don't have to leave the Catholic Church to worship this way."[52]

Participants frequently speak of the tremendous sense of freedom, love, family, and community they feel in Catholic Charismatic prayer groups, rallies, and events. For many alienated Latinos/as, Charisma in Missions functions like a surrogate family, an emotional and social resource center when times are tough. This is why Charisma in Missions has been especially successful in attracting youth.

Today Charisma in Missions is still actively bringing spiritual renewal to the Catholic Church and Latino Catholicism throughout the U.S. and Latin America. The hierarchy of the church—from Pope Francis on down to local bishops and priests in the U.S.—is much more supportive of Charisma in Missions and the CCR than at any time in its history. Charisma in Missions is still growing, although what will happen in the wake of

---

51. Esther J. Garzón, *Evangelization, Mission of the Church* (Montebello, CA: Charisma in Missions, n/d); Esther J. Garzón, *Methodology: Fundamental Initial Course of Evangelization* (Montebello, CA: Charisma in Missions, n.d.).

52. Kahler and Díaz as cited in Ramírez, "Getting That Old-Time Religion," B1, B6.

Kramar's passing is uncertain. Yet followers and leaders remain hopeful that the work she pioneered in the Catholic Church will not only continue but blossom into new movements across the U.S. and around the world.

Conclusion: The Significance of Charisma in Missions

This chapter challenges the assumption that Charisma in Missions is an outgrowth of the Catholic Charismatic Renewal in the United States. Charisma in Missions was founded in 1972 by two Pentecostal missionaries, Glenn and Marilynn Kramar, to bring about spiritual renewal and reformation in the Roman Catholic Church. The Kramars intentionally brought Pentecostal programs, tactics, and rituals into the Latino/a Catholic community and reconfigured them in light of their Catholic theology and audience. Next to the *Cursillo* movement, Charisma in Missions has been one of the most important, if overlooked, misunderstood, and underestimated forces for spiritual renewal in Latino/a Catholicism. It has not only served as a bulwark against Protestant and Pentecostal proselytism, but it has also been the largest tributary feeding into the North American Latino/a Catholic Charismatic movement over the last three decades. It has grown from just two people in 1972 to a movement based in Los Angeles that has since then touched the lives of millions of Catholics throughout the U.S. and Latin America. Much of Charisma in Mission's growth is due to its focus on small group meetings, lay leader mobilization, leadership training seminars, personal evangelism, youth programs, enthusiastic and experiential worship services, greater opportunities for women in lay ministry, and its emphasis on spirituality, and an experiential relationship with Jesus Christ and the Holy Spirit. Charisma in Missions has created one of the few spaces in many Latino/a Catholic Churches where women and young people can exercise voice and leadership. These factors along with its decentralized approach may help begin to explain why it has been able to spread throughout the United States, Mexico, Puerto Rico, and Latin America.

Engaging Landscapes

San Francisco Bay Area Protestants in the Progressive Era

Douglas Firth Anderson

During the summer of 1911, a hiker in Yosemite National Park reflected that "we climb the stairs God built on our own feet, listening for the next trickle of water, and drinking at every one—for they are fountains of youth." Words of John Muir? That summer, his *My First Summer in the Sierra* was published. At one rhapsodic point in his book, Muir commented,

> No Sierra landscape that I have seen holds anything truly dead or dull, or any trace of what in manufactories is called rubbish or waste; everything is perfectly clean and pure and full of divine lessons. This quick, inevitable interest attaching to everything seems marvelous until the hand of God becomes visible; then it seems reasonable that what interests Him may well interest us. When we try to pick out anything by itself, we find it hitched to everything else in the universe.[1]

The hiker, though, was not the California-based founder of the Sierra Club and "apostle" of the Sierras. Muir spent much of 1911 outside of California. (Meanwhile, San Francisco's leaders developed their case for creating a reservoir in the Hetch Hetchy Valley of Yosemite National Park.) The rhapsodic hiker was the Reverend Arthur P. Vaughan (1877–1952), editor of the *Pacific Presbyterian*.[2]

---

1. Muir, *My First Summer in the Sierra* (New York: Penguin, 1997) 157.
2. Arthur Pierce Vaughan, "Fountains of Youth in Yosemite," San Francisco weekly, *Pacific Presbyterian* (August 10, 1911) 7.

Muir's theistically-infused sensibilities about the natural world were rooted in his Protestant upbringing (Scots Calvinist Campellite).[3] It is not surprising that the Rev. Vaughan should echo Muir (he also quoted Muir in his article). Late twentieth-century developments in environmentalism, though, have obscured the movement's historic indebtedness to Christianity.[4]

Recovering Muir's Protestant roots has developed in tandem with a wider recovery of environmentalism's connections to religion.[5] Historian Mark R. Stoll is at the leading edge of this recovery.[6] In *Inherit the Holy Mountain*, his most recent work, Stoll identifies Reformed Protestantism in particular as formative in environmentalism's rise in America.

Stoll is not saying that only those in the Reformed tradition (Congregationalists, Presbyterians, and others) contributed significantly to environmentalism. Neither is he claiming that Reformed Protestants generally were conservationists. Rather, he identifies a matrix of theological perspectives and sensibilities that shaped the childhoods of "a high proportion of leading figures in environmental history."[7] For the Reformed, it has been axiomatic that nature—God's handiwork—points to its Creator, and it is both a proper setting for engaging with God as well as a fitting

---

3. See Ronald H. Limbaugh, "The Nature of John Muir's Religion," *Pacific Historian* 29 (1985) 16–29; and Donald Worster, *A Passion for Nature: The Life of John Muir* (New York: Oxford University Press, 2008) 8, 36–39, 101, 202, 214, 374, 415, 458.

4. For example, see Lynn White, Jr., "The Historical Roots of Our Ecologic Crisis," *Science* 155 (1967) 1203–7; Stephen Fox, *The American Conservation Movement: John Muir and His Legacy* (Madison: University of Wisconsin Press, 1985); Hal K. Rothman, *The Greening of a Nation: Environmentalism in the United States since 1945* (Fort Worth: Harcourt Brace College, 1998).

5. See, for example, Donald Worster, "John Muir and the Roots of American Environmentalism," in *The Wealth of Nature: Environmental History and the Ecological Imagination*, ed. Donald Worster (New York: Oxford University Press, 1993) 184–202; David N. Livingstone, "The Historical Roots of Our Ecological Crisis: A Reassessment," *Fides et Historia* 26 (1994) 38–55; Lynn Ross-Bryant, "Sacred Sites: Nature and Nation in the U.S. National Parks," *Religion and American Culture* 15, no. 1 (2005) 31–62; Jared Farmer, *On Zion's Mount: Mormons, Indians, and the American Landscape* (Cambridge, MA: Harvard University Press, 2008).

6. See, in order of publication, Stoll's *Protestantism, Capitalism, and Nature in America* (Albuquerque: University of New Mexico Press, 1997); "Review Essay: The Quest for Green Religion," *Religion and American Culture* 22, no. 2 (2012) 265–74; *Inherit the Holy Mountain: Religion and the Rise of American Environmentalism* (New York: Oxford University Press, 2015).

7. Stoll, *Inherit the Holy Mountain*, 2

subject for study. "Reformed Protestants were fond of thinking of nature as a holy book to be read," he notes.[8] Jonathan Edwards was merely the most famous American exemplar of Reformed Protestants seeking God in solitude in nature "far from the works of fallen humanity."[9] Moreover, loving, improving, and stewarding nature has been a common pathway of glorifying God for the Reformed. Stoll argues that in the nineteenth century, a "Calvinist Crescent from Baltimore through Philadelphia and New York to Boston" birthed American landscape art, various institutions promoting natural science and agricultural education, and city, state, and national parks.[10] Then in the Gilded Age and Progressive Era, "Presbyterian presidents, secretaries of the Interior and Agriculture, politicians, and journalists transformed Congregational conservation" into what became environmentalism.[11] "From Calvinism," argues Stoll, "American environmentalism acquired many traits that would distinguish it, from its moralism to its suspicion of humans in the landscape to its urgent evangelism."[12] Only after about 1960 does the Reformed influence in environmentalism dissipate, in his view. All in all (and with plentiful examples such as John Muir offered in support), this amounts to what I will call, for convenience, the Stoll thesis.

Whether the Stoll thesis is largely sustainable remains to be seen. It is so broad in its scope and imprecise in identifying who is Reformed that it runs into problems in its details the further it is developed. However, it has enough plausibility enough of the time to invite engagement. How important were Protestants, especially the Reformed, in the rise of more ecological engagements with the American landscape? I cannot adequately address this broad question here. I can, however, provide some answers to a far narrower question: what perspectives on California's landscapes did Anglo-American Protestants of the San Francisco Bay Area have during the Progressive era (1900–1920)?

Why such a circumscribed region, group, and era? First, since Muir is important to the Stoll thesis, analyzing the regional Protestant community which knew Muir best can help confirm or adjust broader generalizations.

8. Ibid., 41.
9. Ibid., 40.
10. Ibid., 266.
11. Ibid., 267.
12. Ibid., 53.

Second, articulate anglophone Protestants were an elite (mostly white, male, middle class, and highly educated). "Prior to 1960," notes historian David A. Hollinger, "if you were in charge of something big and had opportunities to influence the direction of the society, chances are you grew up in a white Protestant milieu."[13] Yet they plausibly spoke for a religious community which emphasized a meritocracy of the Spirit. Urban Anglo-American Protestants had an infrastructure of institutions. Although disparate, often competitive, and occasionally combative, Protestants in and around San Francisco, Oakland, Berkeley, and Alameda nonetheless related to each other as members of a loose-knit religious community—a "spiritual tribe," to borrow the phrase of sociologist Nancy Tatom Ammerman—through congregations, missions, Sunday school conventions, revivals, colleges, seminaries, and denominational weeklies.[14] Many of these institutions could be traced back to the Gold Rush era, when San Francisco was the center of West Coast Protestantism. By the Progressive era, the denominational press in particular—like the Rev. Vaughan's *Pacific Presbyterian*—gave regional Protestantism a public voice.[15]

Finally, the Progressive era brought to fruition reformist concerns of the Gilded Age—including conservation, as detailed in the Stoll thesis. During the Progressive era, when John Muir was recognized throughout the nation as a leading conservationist, the Bay Area Protestant community was particularly preoccupied by two interconnected landscapes: sociocultural and natural. Religiously, Protestants were a decided minority in the region. Immediately prior to the region's infamous catastrophic earthquake and fire, there were roughly 32,000 Protestants out of an urban population of some 540,000.[16] Their numerical marginality fed their strenuous efforts

13. David A. Hollinger, *After Cloven Tongues of Fire: Protestant Liberalism in Modern American History* (Princeton: Princeton University Press, 2013) ix.

14. Nancy Tatom Ammerman, *Sacred Stories, Spiritual Tribes: Finding Religion in Everyday Life* (New York: Oxford University Press, 2014) 10, 300–302.

15. On Bay Area Protestantism during the Progressive era, see Douglas Firth Anderson, "Through Fire and Fair by the Golden Gate: Progressive Era Protestantism and Regional Culture," PhD diss., Graduate Theological Union, 1988. On the regional Protestant press, see Anderson, "*Pacific*," in *Popular Religious Magazines of the United States*, edited by P. Mark Fackler and Charles H. Lippy (Westport, CT: Greenwood, 1995) 373–80.

16. For a detailed discussion of the 1906 statistics and of the Bay Area in comparison with other U.S. urban areas, see Douglas Firth Anderson, "'We Have Here a Different Civilization': Protestant Identity in the San Francisco Bay Area, 1906–1909," *Western Historical Quarterly* 23 (1992) 206–9.

to assert a moral custodianship over the Bay Area's sociocultural landscape. The shock of earthquake and fire (1906), the political turmoil over labor union politics and graft in San Francisco (1906–1909), welcoming the world to a rebuilt San Francisco at the Panama-Pacific International Exposition (1915), and the Great War dominated much of the public thought and activity of regional Protestants. Even so, California's engaging natural landscape could not be entirely ignored. Indeed, for some Protestants the regional natural and sociocultural landscapes were intertwined in ways that arguably presaged "integral ecology."[17] In engaging these landscapes, Protestants found the region paradoxically exhilarating and troubling.

The Rev. Vaughan's camping in Yosemite and the publication of Muir's *My First Summer in the Sierra* were not the only things Bay Area Protestants noted in 1911. In the early spring, ex-president Theodore Roosevelt made a visit to the region. In addition to delivering the Charter Day address at the University of California in Berkeley, he also delivered five lectures on "Realizable Ideals." The series, part of the region's commemoration of the tercentenary of the King James translation of Bible, was sponsored by the Earl endowment of the Pacific Theological Seminary (Congregational), Berkeley.[18]

In his lectures, Roosevelt, a lifelong member of the Reformed Church in America, sketched a biblically informed moral landscape.[19] Although he had famously met with Muir in Yosemite a few years earlier, the "wilderness warrior" did not stress the natural world's role in moral formation.[20] However, among the local reflections on the lectures, there was at least one Protestant who assumed that the moral landscape was "hitched to" the

---

17. Muir's previously quoted ecological insight—that "when we try to pick out anything by itself, we find it hitched to everything else in the universe"—is implicit in Pope Francis' use of the term "integral ecology," which encompasses "human and social dimensions" as well as natural. See Pope Francis, *Laudato Si': On Care for Our Common Home* (Huntington, IN: Our Sunday Visitor, 2015) 93.

18. Roosevelt, *Realizable Ideals (The Earl Lectures)* (San Francisco: Whitaker & Ray-Wiggin, 1912).

19. Robert Bolt, "The Religion of Theodore Roosevelt," *Theodore Roosevelt Association Journal* 19 (1993) 4–7. Stoll, *Inherit the Holy Mountain*, 151, erroneously claims that Roosevelt was Presbyterian.

20. Douglas Brinkley, *The Wilderness Warrior: Theodore Roosevelt and the Crusade for America* (New York: Harper Perennial, 2010) 542–47.

social, domestic, and physical landscapes. Lucia Chase Bell (1848–1938) urged *Pacific Presbyterian* readers that "Children should learn that the Bible country ... was real, real as California, and much like it ... ." For her, it was a "realizable ideal" to meld religious experience with modern technique—"a system of grade work in Bible study for the home"—so that the moral landscape of the Bible could engage in individuals' imagination the multiple landscapes of California.[21]

Bell's concern that the "Bible country" should parallel "real" California reflected in part a collective anglophone Protestant consciousness of California's engaging natural landscape and climate. While the focus of that consciousness was fluid—now the Bay Area itself, now the Sierras, now the entire state—Progressive era Protestants were attuned, like residents in general, to the region's allure.

Three distinctive markers of the regional natural landscape then and now are Yosemite Valley (by then part of a national park), the Big Trees (giant sequoias and coast redwoods), and the Sierra Nevada Mountains. Muir himself was not the first to moralize and sacralize these markers; during the Civil War, the Rev. Thomas Starr King (a Universalist-Unitarian) had done so.[22] Arguably, Muir was not only following larger trends but also a local Protestant tradition in evoking religious sensibilities about California's mountains and trees. Recall A.P. Vaughan's 1911 comment that he was climbing "the stairs God built." Then there was John Wright Buckham (1864–1945). Theologian at the Pacific Theological Seminary, he termed Yosemite "the very house of God and gate of Heaven" on a bright day.[23] Oakland Congregationalist pastor Herbert A. Jump (1875–1934) offered a lengthy "spiritual interpretation" of Yosemite.[24] Advertisements for Yosemite were not uncommon in the denominational press; in 1909, a Yosemite Valley Chautauqua featured not only several regional clergy but also Muir himself.[25]

---

21. *Pacific Presbyterian* (April 13, 1911) 5.

22. Sandra Sizer Frankiel, *California's Spiritual Frontiers: Religious Alternatives in Anglo-Protestantism, 1850–1910* (Berkeley: University of California Press, 1988) 18–31; and Richard Peterson, "Thomas Starr King in California, 1860–64: Forgotten Naturalist of the Civil War," *California History* 49 (1990) 12–21, 79–80.

23. *Pacific* (San Francisco Congregational Churches weekly, June 2, 1915) 7.

24. Herbert Atchinson Jump, *The Yosemite: A Spiritual Interpretation* (Boston: Pilgrim, 1916).

25. *California Christian Advocate* (San Francisco Methodist Episcopal Church weekly, May 13, 1909) 20.

Carrie Judd Montgomery (1858–1946), an Oakland proponent of holiness, faith healing, and premillennialism, transfigured the redwoods into moral actors in the New Creation. In her poem "Primeval Redwoods," she limned their "weighty sermons" that pointed to heaven, taught "holy patience," and exuded priestly incense:

> With mission new in God's restored, new earth,
>
> Ye still shall rear your heads, and join the song
>
> Which morning stars voiced on Creation's day . . . .[26]

To reflect on the Sierra's timeless strength and purity, Presbyterian Vaughan also turned to verse:

> All night their granite pillars
> > Bear up the smothering tent
> Of infinite black above me—
> > I sleep at their feet content.
> They cradle me safe in mosses,
> > They gather the stars for my sky,
> And choirs of pines croon over me
> > The mountains' lullaby.
> How old they are,
> How cold they are,
> Those far heights unattained;
> And stars sweep low
> O'er fields of snow,
> And the winds run unrestrained:
> God's peace is there;
> No noise, no care;
> Nor dust, nor sin have stained.[27]

More broadly, Congregationalist Buckham thought that California's land and climate had a powerful and largely beneficent allure: "the very climate and its call, if not to the wild, at least to life in the open," pulled

---

26. Carrie Judd Montgomery, "Primeval Redwoods," in *Heart Melody* (Oakland: Triumphs of Faith, 1922) 41–42.

27. Arthur Pierce Vaughan, "Sierra Song," *Pacific Presbyterian* (July 27, 1911) 8.

families to meander "on the hills, or under the red woods [sic], or along the seashore, where Nature weaves about the [family] circle its spell of harmony and beauty!"[28] The Rev. John E. Stuchell (1870–1948, Presbyterian) went further: "[T]his is an outdoor country, and if religion is to dominate it, it must be an outdoor religion, adapted to it, not one depending upon an architecture borrowed from northern Europe."[29]

Notwithstanding the Stoll thesis, conservation was not a major issue in the era's regional Protestant press. Indeed, as the public furor over whether or not to dam the Hetch Hetchy Valley in Yosemite National Park rose and fell, local Protestants as Protestants were largely silent on the issue.[30] (On other issues, they were anything but silent.[31])

It was only a minority among Bay Area Protestants that regularly drew attention to California's natural landscape. Yet, in that minority Congregationalists and Presbyterians predominated. Thus, insofar as the Stoll thesis asserts an affinity of Reformed Protestants for conservation, much of the evidence from Progressive era Bay Area Protestantism supports it.

Further regional evidence, though, underscores Stoll's imprecision as to who and what was or was not "Reformed." The regional Protestant commentators on natural California tended to be "cosmopolitan" liberalizers inclined toward immanentist understandings of the divine or, as in the case of Muir himself, post-Reformed (that is, discernably Reformed or Protestant in thought even if un- or other-affiliated as adults).[32]

Two liberalizing Bay Area Protestants who were outspoken conservationists were Joseph LeConte and William F. Badé. LeConte (1823–1901) moved to Berkeley to join the University of California's faculty as professor of geology, botany, and natural history in 1869. He soon gained a national reputation as a neo-Lamarckian proponent of theistic evolution.[33] He also

---

28. *Pacific* (October 7, 1909) 5.

29. *Pacific Presbyterian* (May 5, 1910) 5.

30. See Robert W. Righter, *The Battle over Hetch Hetchy: America's Most Controversial Dam and the Birth of Modern Environmentalism* (New York: Oxford University Press, 2005).

31. See Douglas Firth Anderson, "'A True Revival of Religion': Protestants and the San Francisco Graft Prosecutions, 1906–1909," *Religion and American Culture* 4 (1994) 25–49; and Anderson, "'An Active and Unceasing Campaign': J. Stitt Wilson and Herronite Socialist Christianity," in *Socialism and Christianity in Early 20th Century America*, edited by Jacob H. Dorn (Westport, CT: Greenwood, 1998) 41–64.

32. Hollinger, *After Cloven Tongues of Fire*, 6, 19, 46.

33. Jon H. Roberts, *Darwinism and the Divine in America: Protestant Intellectuals and*

became an important part of the California's scientific community. This regionally distinct group particularly concentrated on field work in the Sierras. Its members, according to historian Michael L. Smith, engaged with environmental interdependence sooner than did their eastern colleagues. LeConte became a close associate of Muir and was a founder of the Sierra Club in 1892.[34] Like Muir, he had a religiously conservative Reformed upbringing, which historian Stoll notes that he left behind as he matured.[35] Yet, unlike Muir, he formally affiliated with the local Protestant community through maintaining membership at First Presbyterian Church, Berkeley.[36]

Curiously, Stoll does not mention William Badé (1871-1936)—perhaps because he was only tangentially Reformed. He was, however, openly Protestant. Born in Minnesota, Badé was Moravian-turned-Congregationalist. After graduate studies at Yale and the University of Berlin, he arrived at the Pacific Theological Seminary in 1902, where he became professor of Old Testament and later dean. He was an outspoken proponent of rigorous historical critical study of the Old Testament.[37] He was also passionate in his love of the natural landscape. He joined the Sierra Club in 1903. As editor of the *Sierra Club Bulletin* (1910-1922), he was heavily involved in resisting the damming of Hetch Hetchy. He was also Muir's literary executor.[38]

Badé and LeConte added further intellectual heft to the other mostly Reformed regional Protestants who valorized the California natural landscape. Nevertheless, the environmentally-engaged group was still small in size and of little influence in reshaping Protestant opinion.

Protestant engagement with California's natural landscape, though, could take forms other than hiking in the Sierras or writing poems about

---

Organic Evolution, 1859-1900 (Madison: University of Wisconsin Press, 1988) 125, 130, 134, 136, 138, 141-42.

34. Michael L. Smith, *Pacific Visions: California Scientists and the Environment, 1850-1915* (New Haven: Yale University Press, 1987) 42-43, 143-65.

35. Stoll, *Inherit the Holy Mountain*, 111-12, 153

36. *Manual of the First Presbyterian Church of Berkeley, California*, 1885, 1896. Stoll, *Inherit the Holy Mountain*, 153, is incorrect to call him Congregationalist in the 1890s.

37. Harland E. Hogue, *Christian Seed in Western Soil: Pacific School of Religion through a Century* (Berkeley: Pacific School of Religion, 1965) 80-81, 246; and Douglas Firth Anderson, "Modernization and Theological Conservatism in the Far West: The Controversy of Thomas F. Day, 1907-1912," *Fides et Historia* 24, no. 2 (1992) 88.

38. William E. Colby, "William Frederic Badé—1871-1936" *Sierra Club Bulletin* pamphlet reprint, 1937; and Righter, *The Battle over Hetch Hetchy*, xi, 64, 74, 75-76, 82, 98, 113, 209, 243.

redwoods. The Rev. Stuchell had exhorted, as noted earlier, that in California an "outdoor religion" was needed, "not one depending upon an architecture borrowed from northern Europe." Stoll discusses landscape artists—including William Keith, Muir's Scots-born friend and "lapsed-Presbyterian environmentalist" Bay Area associate.[39] However, Stoll does not consider architecture and architects. A minority of Bay Area Protestants—mostly non-Reformed and some on or beyond the edge of Protestantism—supported a more "outdoor" aesthetic. They did this through constructing new churches and other religious buildings in "Mediterranean" architectural styles that emphasized tiling, stucco, and light, or in Arts and Crafts eclecticism that featured local stone and wood.[40]

In the Methodist *California Christian Advocate*, Oakland architect C.B. Ripley promoted, among other things, the Mission Revival style.[41] Even before Ripley's recommendation, St. Mark's Episcopal Church, Berkeley built their new church in this style (1902). The 1911 post-earthquake San Francisco First Methodist Church structure blended Mission with Tudor style.[42]

For Bay region Protestants, though, Arts and Crafts architecture proved more popular than Mission. Three non-Reformed Bay Area churches became monuments of Arts and Crafts: the San Francisco Church of the New Jerusalem (Swedenborgian, 1894), the Berkeley Unitarian Church (1898), and the First Church of Christ, Scientist, Berkeley (1910).[43]

Further, the Mediterranean and Arts and Crafts styles were prominent in architect Julia Morgan's Progressive era work for Protestants. Morgan (1872–1957) was a native of San Francisco and raised in Oakland's First Baptist Church (having a Northern Baptist background was not necessarily the same as having a Reformed background). She majored in engineering

39. Stoll, *Inherit the Holy Mountain*, 148.

40. On the styles, see Peter W. Williams, *Houses of God: Religion, Region, and Architecture in the United States* (Urbana: University of Illinois Press, 1997) 249, 270–71, 277.

41. *California Christian Advocate* (January 16, 1908) 15. For other articles by Ripley on church architecture, see *California Christian Advocate* (August 22, 1907) 14; (October 3, 1907) 14; (October 24, 1907) 15; (January 2, 1908) 17; (March 18, 1908) 14.

42. *Seventy-Five Years of St. Mark's* (Berkeley: St. Mark's Episcopal Church, 1952) 12–13; Ruth Hendricks Willard and Carol Green Wilson, *Sacred Places of San Francisco* (Novato, CA: Presidio, 1985) 16–18.

43. Willard and Wilson, *Sacred Places of San Francisco*, 70–73; Karen J. Weitze, "Utopian Place Making: The Built Environment in Arts and Crafts California," in *The Arts and Crafts Movement in California: Living the Good Life*, edited by Kenneth R. Trapp (Oakland: Oakland Museum, 1993) 56–62; Williams, *Houses of God*, 277–78, 293.

at the University of California, worked for local architect Bernard Maybeck, completed the architectural program of the Ecole des Beaux-Arts in Paris (she was the first woman to be admitted), and opened her own architectural firm in San Francisco in 1904. Like Muir, Morgan was post-Protestant as an adult, her work arguably becoming her religion. It was also some of her Progressive era work that kept her informally tied to the Protestant community of her youth. At the suggestion of Phoebe Apperson Hearst (a Protestant adherent, and the link for Morgan's later work for Hearst's son William Randolph), Morgan designed the Asilomar Conference Center (1913) for the Pacific Coast Young Women's Christian Association (YWCA). On thirty acres of Hearst-donated coastal land adjacent to Pacific Grove (a town which had grown up around a Methodist camp ground), Morgan created multiple structures of local stone, wood beams, and shingles set among the redwoods and Monterrey pines in a way that interwove natural and built landscapes.[44] In addition, Morgan designed other structures for the YWCA, including the Oakland YWCA building (1913). For the latter, she turned to Mediterranean styling to bring outdoor light into the heart of the building. Her earlier St. John's Presbyterian Church, Berkeley (1908–1910) was Arts and Crafts.[45] In her Progressive era Protestant architecture, Morgan found ways to engage multiple landscapes—built, natural, and spiritual—through enhancing their convergence experientially.

Overall, however, regional Protestants were divided in engaging the two perceived primary landscapes: natural and social. Lucia Chase Bell's desire that for children the "Bible country" should be as real as "real" California, John Wright Buckham's conviction that California's natural environment called for a "life in the open" for families, and John E. Stuchell's declaration that California was "an outdoor country" which demanded an "outdoor religion" were "placed" moral perceptions. In fact, concerns about the moral interconnections between California's natural and sociocultural landscapes were widespread among the Bay Area Protestants—far more so than explicit support for conservation.

On the one hand were those like Buckham and Stuchell who saw California's landscapes as more promising than perilous. Baptist (and Berkeley

---

44. Oakland First Baptist Church, *One Hundredth Anniversary: First Baptist Church, Oakland, California, 1854-1954* (Redwood City: 100th Anniversary Committee, 1954) 17; Sara Holmes Boutelle, *Julia Morgan, Architect*, rev. ed. (New York: Abbeville, 1995) 7-49, 87-95; *Pacific Baptist* (McMinnville, OR, Northern Baptist weekly, August 2, 1913) 16-17.

45. Boutelle, *Julia Morgan*, 88, 95-99, 69-73.

university librarian) the Rev. C. M. Jones saw no difficulty linking California with the Holy Land and God's glorification:

> Land like ours the place where he,—
> Christ-Child there in Palestine,—
> Came to His nativity;
> Land of smiling sky and sea;
> Verdant hill and fruitful lea;
> Climate his, like ours, benign!
> Came to home of olive, vine,
> Citron, fig and all the rest;
> Clouds that weep and skies that shine,
> California, like to thine;
> Claim thou too this Christ divine,
> Glorify him with thy best![46]

English-born the Rev. Robert Whitaker (1863–1944), pastor of Oakland's Twenty-Third Avenue Baptist Church and an outspoken Christian Socialist and pacifist, was prepared to go further than Jones:

> [T]here is no field for religious effort more appealing and more inspiring than California. . . . Half of the irreligiousness of California is itself religious. Idealism springs naturally in this lovely land of ours. There may be souls who can traverse our Sierra, and overlook our incomparable valleys with no sense of the divine. But no book of devotions is half so eloquent of God as a thousand scenes upon which I have looked from the Siskiyous to the sea by San Diego. . . . The weakling may perish here if his imported religion is a mere veneer. But the Abrahamic soul may still find its Canaan in the west, beside the waters of the world's last Mediterranean, the "Great Sea" of the morrow, and "chosen people" of God had never nobler conquest before them, nor promise of larger reward than here.[47]

For Whitaker and some other Protestants, the extraordinary natural landscape of the Bay Area and California transfigured the sociocultural

---

46. Charles Melancthon Jones, "California's Christmas," *Pacific Baptist* (December 19, 1914) 11.

47. Robert Whitaker, "Is California Irreligious?" *Sunset* 16 (1906) 384–85.

landscape. The California Dream—a Western variant of the American Dream—offered, in their view, millennial promise.[48]

Other regional Protestants were inclined to see the California Dream as less millennial than nightmarish. For Bell and others, the region's natural and sociocultural landscapes were at best in tension, or at worst, mutually seductive. The Rev. Marion R. Drury (1849–1939), for example, articulated what most Protestant immigrants to the Bay Area seemed to key in on: "We have here a different civilization from that found east of the Rocky Mountains." Sent by the United Brethren in 1907 to organize a congregation, Drury was sensible of a "dominant worldliness" and "cosmopolitan life" in the sociocultural landscape that undercut receptivity to the divine either there or in the natural landscape.[49]

Stanford University's Chaplain, the Rev. D. Charles Gardner (1871–1948, Episcopal) was more pointed than Drury: "We face an exaggerated individualism which is unsocial, a Latin-like love of pleasure, masses of men and women superficially educated, and frankly in love with rag-time music, movie morals and the Sunday Supplement type of literature, an educated group out of sympathy with organized Christianity, a climate which effects character and conduct, a prosperity turning to grossness."[50] Most likely the climate Gardner alluded to was sociocultural rather than natural. Perhaps, though, nature was an implied ground for the cultural climate.

Oakland native W.N. Friend (1870–1934), pastor of Howard Presbyterian Church, San Francisco, was less ambiguous about the overlap of Bay Area society and nature. With studied alliteration, he declared in 1913 that, as a Protestant pastor in San Francisco, "One strives against pagan and proletariat and pioneer amidst the beautiful, the bizarre and the beastly."[51] Another Presbyterian, E.A. Wicher (1872–1957), a professor of New Testament at the San Francisco Theological Seminary, was less alliterative, but more explicit:

> The writer of this article is moved only by an intense love for San Francisco, for the beauty of her hills and the sea, her light of

---

48. Kevin Starr, *Americans and the California Dream, 1850–1915* (New York: Oxford University Press, 1975); and Starr, *Inventing the Dream: California through the Progressive Era* (New York: Oxford University Press, 1985).

49. *Pacific* (May 21, 1908) 3.

50. D. Charles Gardner, "Service to the Social Order," in *Religious Progress on the Pacific Slope*, edited by Charles S. Nash and John Wright Buckham (Boston: Pilgrim, 1917) 299.

51. *Pacific* (April 16, 1913) 3.

evening through the Golden Gate; most of all for her men and women, who are so strong-handed, and yet oftentimes so weak in their strength. He loves this city so much that he hates everything that injures her; he hates her saloons and brothels and Barbary Coast, hates her spurious religions and pseudo intellectualism, her corruption in politics and her indifference to moral judgments.[52]

Drury, Friend, and Wicher bespoke a long-standing anxiety among many Bay Area Protestants: how to reshape the "different civilization" of the region lest it keep Protestants culturally marginalized. In the wake of the San Francisco fire and earthquake, Wicher forthrightly restated a long-standing Protestant perception of the regional sociocultural landscape:

For, if the Church in the East has a hard warfare against materialism, the Church in the West has the same warfare against an enemy more strongly entrenched and with inferior resources of men and weapons. California was originally a Spanish Roman Catholic territory, in which the few settlers lived without care and responsibility, and the good fathers exploited the Indians. San Francisco has remained a city predominantly Roman Catholic to this day. Anglo-Saxon settlement began with a gold rush . . . But the men who thirsted for the gold did not commonly devote much of it to the causes of religion—and in San Francisco to-day the wealth is not, generally speaking, in the hands of religious men.[53]

In short, for the Anglo-American Protestants of the Bay Area, the region was a "different civilization" in part because it was Catholic, in part because it was a secular "instant city" of the Gold Rush.[54] Protestantism had always been marginal within the Bay region. During the Progressive era, even though the natural landscape shook, the religious landscape's tilt away from Protestantism did not shift.

In light of the sociocultural landscape, then, at least some Protestants worried that the region's engaging natural landscape was a temptation as much as a blessing. The less sanguine ones, such as George E. Burlingame (1870–1934), pastor of First Baptist Church, San Francisco, viewed "the charming climate" as a substantial foundation for California's "shameful

---

52. Edward Arthur Wicher, "Religion at the San Francisco Exposition," *Continent* 46 (September 9, 1915) 1204.

53. Edward Arthur Wicher, "Training Presbyterian Ministers," *New York Observer* 85 (August 8, 1907) 177–78.

54. See Gunther Barth, *Instant Cities: Urbanization and the Rise of San Francisco and Denver* (New York: Oxford University Press, 1975).

distinction" of having no Sunday laws. In Burlingame's view, "the Spanish Romanists" and "275 rainless days in the year, with a mean average temperature of 55 degrees, fixed the character of popular Sunday observance as a day of feasting and carnivals and reveling and sport."[55] More sanguine Protestants such as Congregationalist John Wright Buckham were nonetheless aware that the regional climate "weakened the home instinct." While "Sunshine without enhances sunshine within," Buckham recognized challenges in how California's natural environment differed from New England's: "Children who do not have to come indoors to get warm, wander farther and get less oversight than in a harsh and unkindly climate. Protection and dependence are less urgent than elsewhere."[56]

In light of the Stoll thesis, what, then, would be fair to conclude about Bay Area Protestants and California's landscapes during the Progressive era? First, John Muir's Protestant-infused rhetoric about the natural landscape resonated with the Protestant community generally. The exceptional climate, coast, mountains, and Big Trees were revelatory of a Creator and of a moral order. Loving nature—especially California's—was not much of a stretch, at least in principle.

Second, though, conservation was not a major concern for most Protestants as Protestants. Given the California Dream, few seemed to see a need to do much rethinking of how much human "improvement" of nature was appropriate, let alone sustainable. Indeed, at the time, what with the business and engineering systems that created, sustained, and expanded such things as the Southern Pacific Railroad, the Hetch Hetchy and Owens Valley water projects, electric power, early automobiles and airplanes, bungalow suburbs, and the mass importing and planting of eucalyptus, orange, and palm trees, California seemed to be "improving" quite nicely—at least in the eyes of many middle-class whites, including most Protestants.[57]

Most Protestants, along with others, could readily support the creation of parks. As Stoll notes, a devout Presbyterian like southern California Congressman William Vandever had no problem sponsoring the 1890 bills that created Yosemite, Sequoia, and General Grant Grove National Parks. What Stoll misses, though, is that Vandever had no conservation record;

---

55. George E. Burlingame, "San Francisco: A Challenge to Evangelical Christianity," *The Standard* 56 (December 26, 1908) 8.

56 *Pacific* (October 7, 1909) 5.

57. See Starr, *Inventing the Dream*; and Jared Farmer, *Trees in Paradise: A California History* (New York: Norton, 2013).

his park bills were at the behest of the Southern Pacific Railroad.[58] Parks were good for recreation—and for fostering tourism for local businesses and the Southern Pacific.

Third, among the Protestant minority who were inclined to conservation, the Reformed tradition broadly defined appears dominant. Stoll is, in this regard, onto something. Notwithstanding his post-Reformed adult life, John Muir did have Reformed allies, from Presbyterians Joseph LeConte, A.P. Vaughan, and J.E. Stuchell to Congregationalists J.W. Buckham and William Badé. He also had, though, non-Reformed who seemed to wish him well, from Baptist C.M. Jones to his own wife, Methodist Louie Strentzel Muir. Indeed, Louie Muir's support suggests that there is probably more evidence of Protestant support—particularly among women—waiting to be tracked down outside of specifically religious sources.[59]

Fourth, Bay Area Protestants were most discomfited by the sociocultural landscape. Indeed, while the California natural landscape might seem Edenic, the sociocultural landscape made many regional Protestants feel "out of Eden" and morally displaced and "homeless."[60] It would take decades for more of them to feel similarly about the altered natural landscape.

Creating and visiting parks did not allay Bay Area Protestant anxieties about their own cultural marginality in the region. (Protestants in southern California at the time had a different relationship with their region.[61]) Burlingame and Buckham's suspicions that the natural landscape was as likely to work against evangelizing the sociocultural environment were moralizing,

58. Stoll, *Inherit the Holy Mountain*, 152–53. Vandever Mountain, 11,947 feet, stands just inside the southern border of Sequoia National Park. On Vandever, see Douglas Firth Anderson, "'More Conscience than Force': U.S. Indian Inspector William Vandever, Grant's Peace Policy, and Protestant Whiteness," *Journal of the Gilded Age and Progressive Era* 9 (2010) 167–96; on Vandever and the Southern Pacific, see Richard J. Orsi, *Sunset Limited: The Southern Pacific Railroad and the Development of the American West, 1850–1930* (Berkeley: University of California Press, 2005) 362–64, 370–71, 573n36.

59. On Louie Strentzel Muir, see Worster, *A Passion for Nature*, 239. For an example of where non-religious sources for Protestant women's support of conservation can be found, see Cameron Binkley, "Saving Redwoods: Clubwomen and Conservation, 1900–1925," in *California Women and Politics: From the Gold Rush to the Great Depression*, edited by Robert W. Cherny, Mary Ann Irwin, and Ann Marie Wilson (Lincoln: University of Nebraska Press, 2011) 151–73.

60. See Steven Bouma-Prediger and Brian J. Walsh, *Beyond Homelessness: Christian Faith in a Culture of Displacement* (Grand Rapids: Eerdmans, 2008) for a bracing ecological and theological analysis of home, homelessness, displacement, and homecoming in this contemporary age.

61. See Anderson, "Modernization and Theological Conservatism," 83–90.

to be sure, but also shrewder than might first appear. In a recent study using county-level data, sociologists Todd W. Ferguson and Jeffrey A. Tamburello argue that "natural amenities" such as "beautiful weather, water, and mountains" are a "spiritual resource" that "compete with traditional local religious organizations." That is, "between two counties with the same levels of recreational opportunities and civic organizations, the county with the greater amounts of coastlines, mountains, and good weather will have lower religious adherence rates." In short, it would appear that the Bay Area's exceptional natural landscape has, in some measureable way, posed a challenge for all institutionalized religion. "The West [and California in particular]," observe Ferguson and Tamburello, "has historically had lower rates of adherence in traditional religious organizations than the rest of the nation. . . . This is *not* because residents of the West are less religious than the rest of the nation. Instead, Americans in the West have another supplier of spiritual goods—the natural environment—to meet their demands for the sacred."[62]

Muir's claim that "the hand of God" becomes visible in Yosemite (a phrase from the Muir quote in the first paragraph of this essay) resonated well with Protestant sensibilities. Ironically, though, Muir found that engaging nature was religion enough for him. Others have followed Muir in this. For Protestants (and other "spiritual tribes" for that matter), the challenge to reconnect formal religion and an appreciation of nature has only grown since the Progressive era. Reformed Protestants Steven Bouma-Prediger and Brian J. Walsh, incisive in assessing the multiple dislocations of this contemporary world, observe that an integral ecology is only sustainable for the long term in religious communities. Not just any religious communities, though. They should be characterized by "journeying homemaking." They should be communities of faithful sojourners who love this world, take care for it, and make a welcoming home in it, yet know that this world is only provisionally home. They are sojourners because they yearn for the true homeland which is "not some other world, but this world redeemed and transfigured" into a New Creation in Jesus Christ.[63] Muir would probably understand what they are talking about.

---

62. Todd W. Ferguson and Jeffrey A. Tamburello, "The Natural Environment as a Spiritual Resource: A Theory of Regional Variation in Religious Adherence," *Sociology of Religion* 76 (2015) 296, 309, 310.

63. Bouma-Prediger and Walsh, *Beyond Homelessness*, 296–97.

The Paradoxes of Life at the U.S.-Mexico Border

A View from Imperial County, California

Barbara A. Wells

THE RESEARCH DISCUSSED HERE is a revision of a part of a full-length study about daughters and granddaughters of Mexican immigrant farmworkers.[1] The particular emphasis here explores the impact of the border on the individuals and families living in the Imperial Valley, located in Imperial County, in the far southeastern part of California. It also captures for readers unaccustomed to the social environment of the borderlands a sense of the unique challenges and paradoxes experienced by those living near the U.S.-Mexico border.

The women I studied were right when they observe their lives were indeed shaped by the border. While a border may be defined simply as a physical and political boundary between two countries, the social and political relations associated with the border are complex. Border scholars typically conceptualize the border as a region (rather than a boundary) that includes both sides of the physical border. This conceptualization captures the dynamic nature of the border and the interrelationship between communities and people on both sides. By this view, the concept of symbiosis or interdependence that transcends national boundaries is key to understanding border regions.[2]

---

1. Barbara A. Wells, *Daughters and Granddaughters of Farm Workers: Emerging From the Long Shadow of Farm Labor* (New Brunswick, NJ: Rutgers University Press, 2013).

2. Oscar J. Martinez, *Border People: Life and Society in the U.S.-Mexico Borderlands* (Tucson: University of Arizona Press, 1998).

The U.S.-Mexican border is a 2,000-mile boundary with settlement concentrated in several twin cities, from San Diego-Tijuana on one side to Brownsville-Matamoros on the other. These twin cities—with the exception of San Diego-Tijuana—are patterned in a similar way, with the Mexico cities larger than their U.S. twins. Further, the U.S. border cities are relatively less prosperous than other U.S. cities while Mexico border cities are relatively more prosperous than other cities in Mexico. On the U.S. side of the border, Latinos are a majority of the population in all border cities except San Diego.

In the Imperial County borderlands, Calexico, California and Mexicali, Baja California are the twin cities. Calexico had a population of 35,273 in 2005, while Mexicali's population was 653,046. Mexicali is located in the Municipality of Mexicali, the Mexican *municipio* or county across the border from Imperial County. Mexicali is the State of Baja California's capital city. In discussing historic development on the U.S.-Mexico border, Norma Fimbres Durazo describes the importance of this particular border region: "[O]ne of the most significant social phenomena that has developed is the migration of people from other regions of Mexico to the Imperial-Mexicali region. Calexico, California, and Mexicali, Baja California, were established by these migratory currents in the early twentieth century. The two cities sit next to one another across the border and have transformed the region into a transborder space with the exchange of goods and capital and an international job market that remains viable today."[3]

The migratory patterns of Mexicans over the past several decades are illustrated in the dramatic growth of the Municipality of Mexicali relative to Imperial County. In 1930, Imperial County had a population of 60,903, which was double Mexicali's population of 29,900. By 1950, the situation had changed markedly with Mexicali's population of 124,362 almost double that of Imperial County with 62,975 residents. In 2000, Mexicali, with a population that had grown to 764,602, was more than five times larger than Imperial County, with a population of 142,361.[4]

Mexicali currently serves as home to a large segment of the agricultural work force in the Imperial Valley. Mexicali residents make up most of the 15,000–18,000 seasonal farm workers who harvest the crops in the

---

3. Norma Fimbres Durazo, "Capitalist Development and Population Growth in the County of Imperial, California, and Mexicali, Baja California," in *Imperial-Mexicali Valleys: Development and Enviornments of the U.S.-Mexican Border Region*, edited by K. Collins (San Diego: San Diego State University Press, 2004) 44.

4. Collins, Introduction to *Imperial-Mexicali Valleys*, ed. Collins, 4.

Imperial Valley every year. These workers generally cross the border daily in anticipation of being hired as day laborers by farm labor contractors. Prospective workers congregate at the border at 4:00 or 5:00 a.m. and board buses that bring them to the fields in Brawley, Holtville, and elsewhere, and return them to the border at the end of the workday.[5] Other individuals cross the border daily to work for Imperial Valley growers and agricultural services businesses on a semi-regular basis in jobs unrelated to harvest. The majority of these migrant farm workers are men, because although paid farm labor typically involved the entire family in rural Mexico, women may find other opportunities in this urban setting.

Border control policies have also served to swell the population of Mexican border cities including Mexicali because U.S. authorities have routinely deported unauthorized individuals whose home villages were in central and southern Mexico to the Mexican side of the U.S.-Mexican border. So, for example, detainees from Oaxaca may be "repatriated" to Mexicali, perhaps 1500 miles from their original home. Many of these people have remained in the border cities, never returning to Mexico's interior.[6]

Authorized Border Crossings

Imperial County is a site of substantial documented border crossing. Its two official ports of entry are known as Calexico and Calexico East. The border crossing in the town of Calexico is the main entry point for pedestrians and personal vehicles. Calexico East is the commercial entry point for this area. The scale of transborder activity is obvious from the numbers. In 2005 when my primary fieldwork was done, pedestrian entries totaled 4,481,014 while 11,846,703 individuals entered the U.S. in personal vehicles.[7] The sheer volume of border crossings raises the question of why so many of these occur. What explains 16 million annual crossings into a sparsely settled, agriculture-oriented county with a total population of less than 150,000? The answers to this question illustrate the interdependence

---

5. Phillip Martin, *Importing Poverty? Immigration and the Changing Face of Rural America* (New Haven: Yale University Press, 2009).

6. David E. Lorey, *The U.S.-Mexican Border in the Twentieth Century: A History of Economic and Social Transformation* (Wilmington, DE: Scholarly Resources, 1999).

7. U.S. Department of Transportation, 2009, "U.S. Border Crossings/Entries by State/Port and Month/Year," RITA: Research and Innovative Technology Administration; Bureau of Transportation Statistics (http://www.transtats.bts.gov).

of cross-border communities in general and the Mexicali-Imperial region in particular.

The Imperial Valley women I studied frequently referred to the impact of the border on their family lives. They described the principal reasons for border crossing—both their own crossings and those of others on both sides of the border—as employment, shopping, education, medical treatment, and family visits.

In turning to border-related actions and interactions, it is relevant to note Carlos Velez-Ibanez's observation that the separation of people from north and south of the border has been "one-sided: the north trying to keep out the south, whereas from the south there was little or no perception of excluding those from the north." This being the case, it is unsurprising that there are a number of rules and regulations that restrict the admission of Mexican residents to the U.S. and limit their stays. At the same time, there are special regulations that enable Mexican nationals living near the border to be deeply involved in the immediate U.S. border region.[8]

Mexican citizens may enter the U.S. with a passport and valid visa or a Border Crossing Card. The Border Crossing Card (BCC) is especially relevant to understanding the transborder relations of the Imperial-Mexicali region. The BCC, also known as a laser visa or a local passport, permits frequent border crossings for Mexican individuals who live in border areas and meet certain requirements. This card allows Mexican nationals to stay in the U.S. for up to 30 days if they remain within 25 miles of the border (75 miles in Arizona). The Border Crossing Card permits entry for personal business or pleasure, but does not permit entry for employment in the U.S.

Embedded in the credit card-sized BCC is a machine-readable biometric identifier (digital fingerprints or photograph) that is checked with every border crossing. Individuals seeking a BCC are required to provide employment-related information and indicate the reason for frequent border crossings. An important criterion to qualify for this card is the ability to "demonstrate that they have ties to Mexico that would compel them to return after a temporary stay in the United States."[9] Because financial stability and employment in Mexico are viewed as important indicators of intent to return to Mexico, the applications of many individuals are not approved. Many Border Crossing Card holders cross the border daily or

---

8. Carlos G. Velez-Ibanez, *Border Visions* (Tucson: University of Arizona Press, 1996) 4.

9. U.S. Department of State, 2010, Border Crossing Card (http://travel.state.gov).

sometimes more than once a day, accounting for a considerable segment of border crossings.

Another group of border crossers are Mexican residents who are legal permanent residents of the United States. In the Imperial-Mexicali border area, the largest group of these individuals are Mexican agricultural workers who became legal U.S. immigrants with the Special Agricultural Worker (SAW) program that was part of the Immigration Reform and Control Act (IRCA) of 1986. For various reasons, many of these chose to return to Mexico to live and to commute daily or weekly to jobs on U.S. farms. These workers are sometimes referred to as "green card commuters."[10] These individuals have the freedom to cross the border at will.

Dynamics of the Border Region

It is said, "Everyone gets what they want from the border." The point is that everyone who lives at the border does so for a reason and benefits from it in some way. The border impinges on the lives of all border region residents, in ways that are surely positive and negative. But overall, there are compelling (and varied) reasons to live in proximity to the border.

The interconnectedness of the border region is illumined here by data from a number of sources, including women's experiences and observations. The transborder connections explored here are those related to shopping, medical services, and education. Border crossing activity related to employment also figured importantly in the experience of the Imperial County women. I explore this subject in depth in another paper. For now, suffice it to say that a consistent theme of women's narratives was the negative economic effects experienced by community residents when workers from "the other side" took local jobs.

Shopping

One of the main opportunities that proximity to the border provides is the opportunity to access goods and services from "the other side." Transborder shopping is a regular feature of U.S.-Mexico border regions. Mexicans shop in the U.S. for reasons related to quality, availability, and price. Martinez refers to these individuals as "binational consumers." Mexican shoppers seek

---

10. Martin, *Importing Poverty*, 66.

higher quality products, many of which are less available in Mexico, including food, clothing, and other consumer goods. U.S. prices are lower than prices in Mexico for some products, especially highly-tariffed imports.[11]

U.S. retailers benefit tremendously by locating near the border. The success of many Imperial Valley retail businesses depends on Mexican shoppers. Shoppers from Mexico do most of their shopping in three commercial areas. First is downtown Calexico. Pedestrian border crossers generally shop in downtown Calexico, where stores are densely packed into a half-dozen city blocks just north of the border crossing. The scale of these commercial establishments varies widely, from larger enterprises such as Sam Ellis, a locally-owned department store, and J.C. Penney, to medium-sized independent groceries and variety stores, to a multitude of small crowded shops selling an assortment of cheap imported goods. Here most customers are Mexicans and business is transacted in Spanish. This section of Calexico has a very Mexican "feel." An American with little experience at the border might well assume they were in Mexico rather than the U.S. Signs in the grocery stores advertise "pollo" and food shops promote "tortas" and "menudo." Receipts for purchases may even be printed in Spanish.

Downtown Calexico offers a broader variety of commercial services than do the other shopping areas. These include insurance brokers, legal firms (specializing in immigration law), and currency exchange. Most striking are the money exchange shops, where Mexican day laborers frequently stop to change their daily wages from dollars to pesos before crossing back to Mexico.

Two miles north of the border is the second main commercial area drawing transborder shoppers. Shopping here requires a vehicle. This area, just off Highway 111, the main road between Calexico and Brawley, has a Walmart as its central feature. Other retailers are a mix of well-known American companies such as Toys R Us and Radio Shack as well as local establishments.

The third main shopping destination is Imperial Valley Mall, a gleaming, new regional mall located nine miles north of the international border. A local Chamber of Commerce official explained to me the presence of this facility saying, "The IV Mall was built because of Mexico—for shoppers from Mexico. No way can the county support this mall." This indoor mall opened in 2005, offering customers air conditioned comfort and access to 80 stores. Most significantly, the mall provides a very typical American

11. Martinez, *Border People*, 77.

shopping experience with major U.S. retailers such as Dillard's, Macy's, Sears, JC Penney, Victoria's Secret, the Disney Store, and Express represented. Nothing in the mix of retailers suggests that the mall is anywhere near the Mexican border. Most Mexican shoppers drive to this mall in privately owned vehicles, but taxis are also frequently seen dropping off people who have presumably crossed the border on foot.

Shoppers from Mexico provide strong support for Imperial County businesses. A survey of the cross-border shopping activity of Mexicali households found that the top three products purchased in the U.S. are clothing, foot wear, and chicken. Other items frequently purchased are appliances, auto parts, and other foods. The representation of license plates from Mexican states in store parking lots provides evidence of the importance of these shoppers. In my best effort to assess the percentage of cars with Mexico license plates in the Walmart parking lot on an ordinary, midweek afternoon, I found around 48% of cars to be from Mexico.

An intriguing point here is that Walmart is an important retailer in Mexico; in fact, it is the largest private employer in the country with 702 stores in 64 cities in 2005. Further, Mexicali—just over the border from Calexico—has two Walmarts. The reasons Mexican shoppers bother to cross the border to patronize this establishment are related to quality and selection. Walmart Mexico, with headquarters in Mexico City, stocks its stores with merchandise oriented toward the Mexican consumer. Mexicans who shop the Calexico Walmart do so for products oriented toward the American consumer and deemed to be more desirable and of higher quality than those available in their local Walmarts. It was not possible to do the same license plate analysis at the Imperial Valley Mall, with its nearly 5,000 parking spaces, but in general, the proportion of cars from Mexico in the parking lot was typically substantial, but lower than the percentage at Walmart.

The presence of so many Spanish-speaking visitors resulted in many jobs requiring bilingual skills. One might assume that if the lack of bilingual skills presents an obstacle to the employment of Latinos, job-seekers are likely to be deficient in English. In fact, it was lack of competence in Spanish that disqualified some women from particular jobs in this border region. Every woman who participated in this research—each of whom was second or third generation Mexican American—was fluent in English. However, not everyone was fluent in Spanish. A few third generation women were not. For example, Helen Estrada is a 28-year old mother of four whose Texas-born parents did not speak Spanish in their home. She has been looking conscientiously for a job, without success. She says, "I know if I did know two languages, I would automatically get a job. Actually, I was rejected twice because I didn't speak Spanish—I wasn't bilingual. Which is understandable, you know. They want somebody who can communicate with more customers."

The Walmart in Calexico is the clearest example of an employer whose hiring practices seem oriented toward appealing to Mexican shoppers. Here facility in Spanish is more important than English competence and job applicants with Mexican cultural traits seem to be favored over Mexican Americans who are more assimilated to American culture. Marta Lujan describes her experience applying for a job at Walmart in Calexico: "I went to pick up an application. I am speaking English, right? The person I am talking to is answering me in Spanish. I think they wanted somebody that was totally Mexican and that maybe just spoke a little bit of English, but their main language was Spanish." She later had an interview at this Walmart. "They ask me questions in Spanish and I answer them back in Spanish." Marta did not get the job and concludes, "I think I was too Americanized. I don't know."

Health Care and Medical Services

Border region residents also cross the international boundary to access health care and medical services. In general, the transborder transaction occurring here is that Mexico residents gain access to higher quality health care in the U.S., while U.S. residents gain access to lower cost health care and medical services in Mexico.

The movement of people from a developing nation to a developed nation for high quality medical care raises complicated issues. One of the community leaders I interviewed in Brawley told me that many women from Mexico come to Brawley to give birth at the local hospital, Pioneers Memorial Hospital. This subject is sensitive, and raises some morally-charged accusations, because these women typically do not pay for the medical care they receive. There is considerable resentment regarding this situation in the locale because the provision of this care depletes local community resources. This official explained that the hospital tries to get grants from the State of California to offset some of the extraordinary costs associated with its location as a border-region hospital, but there is limited assistance available. In talking about this situation, the women I interviewed pointed to the closing of the hospital in Calexico as evidence of the stress on the medical system caused by border crossers. The hospital in Calexico had provided a substantial amount of care to Mexican border crossers; the conventional wisdom was that as a direct result, the hospital could not control costs, was not financially viable, and had to shut down. They worry that they too could lose their local hospital. Both Pioneers Memorial Hospital in Brawley and El Centro Regional Medical Center accept Mexican patients who are at risk if they fail to receive medical care. This is consistent with their legal responsibility to provide emergency care to all, regardless of ability to pay. This includes providing childbirth services to pregnant women whose labor has advanced beyond the initial stages. Individuals who are not at risk are not provided care.

A Mexican woman might also be motivated to give birth at one of the Imperial Valley hospitals because the child would be born a United States citizen. None of the women in my sample or the community professionals I interviewed expressed resentment related to the matter of citizenship. Rather, their entire concern revolved around the depletion of this community's limited financial resources.

A principal reason for U.S. to Mexico border crossings is accessing lower cost health care and pharmaceuticals. Many U.S. citizens, especially retirees, buy their medications and receive medical, dental, and optical care in Mexico at prices far lower than in the U.S. For many retirees, this represents an economic strategy that permits them to stretch their fixed incomes.

An estimated 15,000 retirees winter in Imperial County.[12] An attractive feature of residing in Imperial County during the winter months is its proximity to Mexico. Most "snowbirds" stay in RV parks, either in mobile homes or in RVs they have driven south from Western Canada or Western states such as Montana, Wyoming, and Colorado. Nearly all of these seasonal residents are Anglos. The quality of facilities and amenities provided in these parks varies widely, but in general, it is accurate to conclude that Imperial County snowbirds spend much less than do retirees who winter just two hours north and west in the Palm Springs area. Some winter residents are frank in saying they come to Imperial County because it is a place where people of modest means can afford to live seasonally. A benefit of winter residence in the county is the ready access it provides to

12. Collins, *Imperial-Mexicali Valleys*, 5.

low-cost prescription drugs and medical services in Mexico. Many retirees are uncomfortable crossing the border at Calexico because Mexicali is a large urban center and is difficult for inexperienced Americans to negotiate. The preferred alternative is driving less than an hour east on I-8 to the southeastern corner of Imperial County and crossing into Algonones from Andrade, California, a small unincorporated community in the Fort Yuma Indian Reservation.

With a population of around 4,000, Algodones represents Mexico on a manageable scale. If Mexicali is intimidating to American visitors, Algodones is not. Visitors from Canada and the United States may park for a small fee in a large secure parking lot provided by the Quechan Indian Nation on the U.S. side and walk across the border to Mexico. Just over the border is the town's compact commercial district, an area that is four blocks square. A frequently stated claim is that there are more pharmacies, doctors, dentists and opticians in Algodones than in any similar four-block area in the world. Immediately inside the border are the pharmacies. Here prices for the most popular prescription drugs are posted on hand-written signs in store windows or on sandwich boards on sidewalks. Pharmacies do a brisk business. Changing U.S. dollars to pesos is unnecessary because dollars are the expected currency for cash purchases. What I found most striking was the sheer number of dental offices. An estimated 350 dentists—including pediatric dentists, orthodontists, endodontists and others—provide care for U.S. and Canadian border crossers. When business is slow, staff from dental offices and optical shops sometimes hawk their services from the sidewalk.

The town of Algodones actively promotes itself as a low-cost provider of quality medical and dental care for retirees from the other side of the border. The website sponsored by the Algodones Tourism and Conventions Committee (COTUCO) states, "[T]his 'border medical land' attracts thousands of Canadians and Americans weekly. What's the big attraction? You can find heavily discounted prescriptions, eye-glasses, and medical and dental care. And, if you listen to your friends in the snowbird RV parks, they can tell you that the care from their Algodones doctor or dentist is as good as anywhere back home."[13] Accessing lower cost health care and medical services in Mexico is obviously appealing to many. My quick and

---

13. Los Algodones Tourism and Convention Committee (COTUCO), 2009, Los Algodones, Mexico (http://www.losalgodonesmexico.com).

incomplete survey of vehicles in the Quechan parking lot found cars from sixteen U.S. states and four Canadian provinces.

Education

Observations at the pedestrian border crossing at First Street in Calexico reveal that a significant number of Mexican children cross the international border daily for school. A few blocks east of the border crossing, in clear view of the fenced barricade that separates Mexico and the United States, is the Calexico Mission School, a 400-student private school associated with the Seventh Day Adventist Church. The school uniforms—all children in burgundy or white shirts, boys in dark trousers and girls in plaid skirts—easily identify students from this school. Approximately 85% of students in this K-12 school are from Mexicali; they cross the border daily from Mexico to the United States and back again.[14] In the mid-afternoon, dozens of students, some walking alone, some clustered in small groups, in some cases older students minding younger ones, can be seen approaching the border crossing. Also in evidence are women—some surely mothers, but also other women, perhaps grandmothers, aunts, or neighbors—who approach the border crossing with one or more younger children in tow. Frequently these women have done some shopping in Calexico and carry one or two plastic bags with them. On hot days, women might carry an umbrella for sun protection. A notable sight is a Mexican woman, umbrella over her head against the beating sun, leading a small troop of uniformed children in single file down First Street. In addition, some parents cross the border by car and pick up their children in the school parking lot.

The description above of the Calexico Mission School and its students differs from the common observation of border scholars that a typical feature of life at the border is the movement of students from Mexico across the border to attend public schools in the U.S.[15] In fact, I also observed a few junior high and high school-aged youths wearing tee shirts and sweatshirts with logos from Calexico public schools and crossing the border from Calexico to Mexicali in the mid-afternoon. I assumed these teens were students returning to Mexicali after a day at school in Calexico. When I asked

---

14. David Steffen, "Economy Decreases Valley Private School Enrollment, Public Schools Grow." *Imperial Valley Press*, October 9, 2009.

15. Oscar J. Martinez, *Border People: Life and Society in the U.S.-Mexico Borderlands* (Tucson: University of Arizona Press, 1998).

my community sources how it is that students from Mexico attend U.S. public schools, the immediate answer was that most of these families have a relative in Calexico. Border-crossing students are enrolled in the school as a member of the household of extended family members in the United States. Schools require proof of residency, but "proof" may misrepresent realities. As a result, classes in Calexico Public Schools are, as one woman said, "overpopulated," meaning large class sizes and crowded classrooms are the norm. Local public schools are less convenient to the international border than is the mission school. Some parents walk an elementary or middle school child across and border and put her or him in a taxi to be dropped off at a city school. After school, that child is either picked up by a taxi or brought to the border or a parent drives across the border and picks up the child at school.

The presence of non-resident students from Mexico in Imperial County Public Schools is a contentious issue in the community. Many believe the schools do not do enough to verify residence. While some rant on this subject in blogs and letters to the editor of the *Imperial Valley News*, cooler heads tend to make two points. The first is that the addition of students from Mexico increases the percentage of English language learners in classrooms, thereby increasing the daunting challenges already faced by classroom teachers. Second, Imperial County children are already some of the most disadvantaged in the State of California. Increasing student numbers function to exacerbate existing inequalities.

The truly dynamic nature of border activity may be seen in that some Mexican American families living in Calexico enroll their children in private schools in Mexicali. These parents perceive the Calexico public schools to be sub-standard, but they cannot afford U.S. private schools. Mexican private schools represent an alternative because they provide a private school experience that is reasonable by U.S. standards. Erica Martinez told me that her brother's family did this for several years. Another woman, a university student at SDSU who did not meet the criteria for inclusion in my research sample, told me that her younger brother was a student at a private school in Mexico. In fact, her mother sometimes made three round trips across the border per day—one "drop off" trip to school in Mexicali, one "pick up" trip home from school, and then sometimes a trip back for after school activities.

Unauthorized Border Crossings

It is unsurprising that in this county with the highest rate of unemployment in California and with many of the women I interviewed unemployed and looking for work, the first concern is jobs. Women did think Mexican citizens were taking "their" jobs, but the people taking them were not the Mexicans from Southern states like Chiapas and Oaxaca who crossed the border illegally in the desert with coyote guides or swam across the All-American Canal. Rather, they were concerned about Mexicali residents who crossed the border legally in the morning, worked in the Imperial Valley (whether or not they were authorized to work), and returned to Mexicali at night to repeat the same routine the next day. The critical distinction here is that these transborder commuters were legal border crossers, but they may be illegal workers. Research by Frank Bean and his colleagues (1994) on the legal status of Mexican commuter workers at the El Paso/Juarez border found that one-third of this group entered the U.S. legally with a BCC, but then worked illegally. In their typology of Mexican border crossers, they refer to this group as legal crossers/illegal workers.[16]

Imperial County as a Site of Border Enforcement

Introducing the subject of border enforcement adds complexity to our analysis. This paper initially framed the construction of the border as a dynamically interconnected region. Conceptualizing the border in this way may lead readers to question the heavy policing of the boundary between partner regions in an integrated social system that transcends national boundaries. These are contradictory impulses. Upon examination, we will see that as a public policy matter, the U.S. has since the early-to-mid 1990s adopted policies that increasingly construct the border to be a heavily guarded barrier between nations, while at the same time promoting the creation of a permeable, dynamic border region.

Historically speaking, U.S.-Mexico border enforcement is relatively new. Historian Patricia Limerick points out that it was European and not Mexican immigration that was an important public issue in the early twentieth century.[17] The Immigration Act of 1924 restricted immigration

---

16. Frank D. Bean, "The United States/Mexico Border: The Effects of Operation Hold the Line on El Paso/Juarez." U.S. Commission on Immigration Reform, 1994.

17. Patricia N. Limerick, *The Legacy of Conquest: The Unbroken Past of the American*

by imposing numerical quotas for European immigration, but not for immigration from Western Hemisphere nations. The only stipulations for Mexican immigration were literacy, the prohibition of contract labor, and an $8.00 head tax. Limerick notes that none of these requirements was strictly enforced.

The Border Patrol was established in 1924 to control both the Mexican and Canadian borders. At this time the international boundaries were divided into "sectors," with border control operations instituted in each sector. With the establishment of the El Centro Sector in 1924, Imperial County has played an important role in border control since the very beginning. At present, the U.S. is divided into twenty sectors, nine of which patrol the U.S.-Mexico border. Approximately 98% of apprehensions occur at the Southwest border. This means that of 1.19 million border patrol apprehensions nationwide in 2005, 1.17 million of these occurred in the sectors at the U.S.-Mexico border[18]

The El Centro Sector covers an area of more than 23,400 square miles. Its agents patrol 71.1 miles of the United States-Mexico international border. Sector operations are conducted through four stations located at Calexico and El Centro in Imperial County, and Indio and Riverside to the north in Riverside County. The Calexico Station administers the international border crossing at Calexico and patrols the city and the 37 miles of international boundary to the east. The El Centro Station patrols the desert and mountains west of Calexico, a span of 34 linear miles. (U.S. Customs and Border Patrol (CBP) 2007).

The Imperial Valley is further involved in border security as the location of one of eight U.S. government-owned detention centers operated by the Office of Detention and Removal, a division of U.S. Immigration and Customs Enforcement (ICE). This facility, the El Centro Service Processing Center (SPC), is a detention center for adult males facing deportation or waiting for a decision on their immigration case. The U.S. Immigration Court responsible for hearing the cases of detained individuals is also located in the detention center. In recent years, the average number of individuals in detention in this facility on any day has been approximately 450.[19] (Fessenden 2010).

West (New York: Norton, 1987).

18. Aaron Terrazas, *Immigration Enforcement in the United States. Migration Policy Institute*, 2008 (http://www.migrationinformation.org).

19. Ford Fessenden, "Immigrant Detention Centers," *New York Times*, Feb. 23, 2010.

One of the strategies mentioned on the El Centro Sector web site for accomplishing its mission is a highly visible deployment of agents. By all observations, this strategy has been successful. Border agents are regularly seen patrolling the county's population centers by a number of different means, including patrols on foot or horseback, by bicycle or motorcycle, in a variety of motor vehicles, and in low-flying helicopters. While the greatest concentration of border control agents is evident in Calexico, I saw border agents in all Imperial Valley cities and towns. Community professionals I interviewed tended to believe most Mexicans in Imperial County were here legally. Their general viewpoint is that people who have managed to cross illegally will quickly move further north where less immigration enforcement occurs. The new checkpoint on Interstate Highway 8 monitors the immigration status of individuals moving east and west. The two long-utilized Border Patrol traffic checkpoints on California Highways 86 and 111 in Imperial County monitor northbound traffic to prevent illegal entrants from leaving the border region. These traffic stops are positioned more than 25 miles north of the border, also serving to deter Mexicans with border crossing cards from leaving their travel zone limit of 25 miles from the border.

Operation Gatekeeper, begun in 1994, reframed the task of border control in Imperial County and reshaped life in the community. The San Diego area had historically been the site of heaviest illegal crossing activity into the U.S. from Mexico. Operation Gatekeeper used a "prevention and deterrence" strategy, preventing many prospective migrants from crossing at the San Diego border by adding officers, enhancing surveillance equipment, and putting up physical barriers.[20] Tightening the border there meant prospective immigrants would need to find another entry point to the U.S.; the illegal immigrant stream would necessarily shift eastward, where migrants would encounter rough mountain terrain and vast deserts. This strategy assumed that harsh geography would serve as a natural deterrent to immigration. What happened instead was that the policy mostly channeled illegal immigration to more hazardous areas, and increasingly, immigrants coped with the increased risk of the journey by using human smugglers, otherwise known as coyotes, who they believed would ensure their safety.[21]

20. Evelyn Nieves, "Illegal Immigrant Death Rate Rises Sharply in Barren Areas," *New York Times* (August 6, 2002).

21 Wayne A. Cornelius, "Death at the Border: Efficacy and Unintended Consequences

The strain on local institutions precipitated by a new federal strategy of border enforcement is especially clear when we consider the statutory responsibilities of coroners and community hospitals. The Imperial County Coroner's Office is responsible under California law for determining the cause of death, identifying the body, and notifying the next of kin when an individual dies in the county. This includes, of course, migrants who die crossing the border. The coroner's office performs autopsies and works closely with the Mexican consulate in Calexico to establish identification. Bodies awaiting identification are stored at Frye Chapel and Mortuary in Brawley. And eventually, many of the dead are buried in the paupers' section of the Park Terrace Cemetery in Holtville. The burial expenses for individuals who have been identified are paid by their families or the Mexican government. Unidentified individuals are buried as John or Jane Doe, with the county covering the costs. By 2004, the county had spent $1.7 million on expenditures related to border deaths.[22]

I visited the Park Terrace Cemetery in 2010. By then, the number of graves in the pauper's field was estimated to be 750. Most were the final resting places of individuals who perished in the desert or drowned in the All-American Canal while attempting to cross the U.S.-Mexico border. Brick-shaped markers provide identification, if known. The pauper's section, located behind a conventional looking grassy cemetery and separated from it by a single barbed wire barrier, is an entirely stark and barren place.

Many who survive the border crossing require medical care. These people are usually brought to the El Centro Regional Medical Center, the hospital closest to the border, where they are most commonly treated for exposure or injuries sustained in crossing the border. According to a hospital official, the El Centro facility provides charity care in the amount of $1.5 million annually for patients assumed to be foreign nationals. The hospital provides emergency care as it is required by law to do, but in most cases, it is not reimbursed from federal border control funds. The Calexico hospital mentioned earlier in this chapter closed in 1995.

For several years, the El Centro Sector had the dubious distinction of being the sector with the highest number of border-crosser deaths.

---

of US Immigration Control Policy," *Population and Development Review* 27, no. 4 (2001) 661–85.

22. Leslie Berestein, "Rugged Routes, Deadly Risks: Migrants Push East to Avoid Fortified Border, with Tragic Results" *San Diego Union-Tribune* (September 29, 2004); Charlie LeDuff, "Just This Side of the Treacherous Border, Here Lies Juan Doe," *New York Times*, September 24, 2004.

California Dreaming

This reflects two deadly scenarios that played out all too often for Mexicans and others crossing illegally into Imperial County, resulting in death from either exposure or drowning. Immigrant deaths due to exposure were rare on the Southwest border prior to 1994, but rose dramatically with the new immigration policy that rechanneled illegal crossings from urban areas to deserts. Heat-related exposure became the leading cause of death by 1998. Journalist Leslie Berestein provides an example of the shift that occurred in immigrant crossings. As illegal border crossings in the San Diego sector became more difficult, an area near the small town of Ocotillo—just over the San Diego County line into Imperial County—became a popular crossing route. Illegal migrants began their trip to the U.S. on a trail near Mexico's Highway 2, between Mexicali and Tijuana. Its popularity derived from the fact that this border area had no surveillance cameras or fencing. This desert trek took migrants over the border and across Davies Valley toward California Highway 98, the southernmost east-west road in the area and in close proximity to the border. As Berestein notes, most of these border crossers had never seen a desert and were "woefully unprepared" for the trip.[23]

Migrants making desert crossings—whether near the San Diego County line or anywhere else in the Imperial desert—are vulnerable to dehydration and heat exhaustion. Wayne Cornelius, a scholar of Mexican immigration, contends that it is impossible to carry enough water for the journey. Summer temperatures in the desert average 112 degrees, with daytime highs often at 120 degrees. He estimates that migrants entering through the Imperial desert will walk 20–30 miles to reach a major road. Many migrants—sometimes on the advice of their coyotes—take just one gallon of water, an amount insufficient for the journey. The Imperial County coroner and his deputies know all too well, however, that sufficient water does not by itself ensure that migrants will not succumb to the elements. Excessive heat can raise a border crosser's body temperature to a level that results in death.[24]

As unlikely as it may sound in the California desert, the second major risk endangering illegal border crossers in the El Centro Sector is death by drowning. An estimated 550 individuals, most of them undocumented immigrants, have drowned in the All-American Canal, an aqueduct that provides the entire water supply for Imperial Valley communities and

---

23. Bernstein, "Rugged Routes."
24. Cornelius, "Death and the Border," 675.

irrigates its agriculture. The All-American Canal is an 82-mile long irrigation canal that carries water from the Colorado River to the Valley. At its widest point, the canal is 200 feet wide, and is at its deepest, 20 feet deep. It originates at the Imperial Diversion Dam, 18 miles northeast of Yuma, Arizona. Fifty-three miles of the canal run parallel to and just north of the U.S.-Mexico border.

From the surface, water in the canal appears deceptively quiet. In fact, the canal moves more than 26,000 cubic feet of water per second and has a strong undercurrent. Immigrants who attempt to cross the canal on a raft or swim across it are frequently unprepared for the perilous conditions they encounter. The concrete-lined sides of much of the canal make it difficult for swimmers in distress to save themselves. Drowning deaths began to rise in 1997 and continued to mount in subsequent years, becoming the major cause of border crossing deaths in the El Centro Sector.[25]

Operation Gatekeeper's success in reducing illegal entries in San Diego and the corresponding effect of increased illegal entries in Imperial County is apparent from immigration statistics. Between fiscal years 1994 and 2000, apprehensions of illegal migrants in the San Diego sector fell 66 per cent, from 450,152 to 151,681. In the same period, El Centro sector apprehensions rose an astonishing 761 percent from 27,654 to 238,126.[26]

The federal response to soaring illegal border activity in Imperial County was a dramatic increase in funding for El Centro Sector operations and additional border agents. In 2002, border-crossing deaths began to decline in Imperial County, and the Tucson sector took over (and continues to hold) the dubious distinction of having the most immigrant crossing deaths annually. This change is believed by many to be associated with a shift of the illegal immigrant stream further east from the now more heavily fortified Imperial County border to the less tightly guarded Tucson sector border in Arizona. Over the course of the past decade, human smugglers have increasingly viewed the Arizona desert as the easiest route for guiding would-be immigrants across the U.S. border. By 2008, 45% of all apprehensions of illegal immigrants in the Southwest border area were in the Tucson sector.[27]

---

25. Elliot Spagat, "Buoys to Be Installed at Canal on Border to Prevent Drownings," *Sarasota Herald Tribune* (June 29, 2011), 3.

26. Cornelius, "Death on the Border," 665.

27. U.S. Customs and Border Patrol, El Centro Sector: Overview. U.S. Dept. of Homeland Security, 2009.

My research participants—all second and third generation Mexican Americans and U.S. citizens—had next to no direct interaction with border enforcement personnel. Certainly, they experienced border control as part of the larger social context in which they lived. They endured traffic checkpoints like everyone else; border patrol circulated through their neighborhoods. But they did not seem to see the border control enterprise as something that related very directly to them. They accepted the border patrol's presence and activities without analysis or critique. In general, their sentiment seemed to be this: we live in a border community, so we need the border patrol to do its job. In fact, the one shared characteristic that allowed these women to be quite disengaged on this subject was the reality that all of them were U.S. citizens; the border patrol was a matter of concern for people who were illegal. This made all the difference.

Conclusion

This chapter captures a fundamental paradox at the Imperial-Mexicali border. On the one hand, U.S. citizens and Mexican citizens with the requisite documents easily cross the border to engage in various economic and social activities. Mexicans cross to the U.S. to shop at Dillard's. Americans cross to Mexico for prescriptions. Mexican children cross to attend the Calexico Mission School. Mexican Americans cross to visit relatives. And on it goes. In addition, some cross border activity reveals connections between Imperial Valley communities and Mexicali that go beyond the decisions and preferences of individuals. For example, marching bands from Mexicali high schools participate in the annual Cattle Call Parade, a major community event in Brawley. Some women I interviewed told me they crossed the border when their children had soccer games in Mexicali.

At the same time, the U.S. government spends billions of dollars on fencing, technology, and personnel to limit the access of some Mexican citizens to the U.S. side of the border. The "war on drugs" is a battle that is fought in large measure at the border. The paradox at the Imperial-Mexicali border is the same paradox that characterizes the entire U.S.-Mexico border. This examination of life on the border reveals contradictory impulses toward what might be called, "a borderless economy and a barricaded border." The present situation is that the border is "more blurred and more sharply demarcated" than in the past.[28] In examining life at the Mexicali-

---

28. Peter Andreas, *Border Games: Policing the U.S.-Mexico Divide* (Ithaca: Cornell

Imperial border, it is ironic to note that NAFTA, the agreement intended to enable North American partners to transcend national boundaries, was instituted in 1994, the same year that Operation Gatekeeper, the program resulting in massive increases in funding for border enforcement, was implemented.

Although the concepts of "border as regional social and economic system" and "border as physical boundary" pull us in different directions, Frank Bean and his colleagues bring these concepts together to see the border "as a complex mixture of both integrating and differentiating processes that are often in tension with one another." This tension predicts that public policy-related discussions of border issues may be contentious. Here, we may expect that individuals with "views that give overriding emphasis to the border as a mostly geographic boundary between sovereign states tend to highlight divergences in state interests and the need for policies that protect these," while individuals with "views that give predominate weight to the border as an area in which northern Mexico and the southwestern United States are inextricable tied together tend to highlight convergences in state interests and the need for policies that foster further integration."[29]

Border-Based Discomforts and Contradictions

I agree with the dominant perspective in the border literature that it is more accurate to describe the border as an integrated region than a boundary between nation states. But a possible consequence of conceptualizing the border as an integrated system is that massive border-based inequalities may be invisible if view this way. The life chances of border-dwellers depend in large measure on whether they live on the U.S. or Mexico side of the border. Americans crossing the border to Mexico for cheap prescriptions represents a different relationship with the border than does Mexicans crossing the border to the U.S. for work because you are desperate to provide for your family. Relations of power are deeply embedded in the borderlands. I believe we can better communicate that transborder exchanges and interactions do not occur on equal terms. For example, the commonly used reference to pairs of border cities such as Calexico-Mexicali or El Paso-Juarez is as "twin towns" or "sister cities." Pablo Vila contends that this language contributes to what he calls "the construction

---

University Press, 2000) 4.

29. Bean, "The United States-Mexican Border," 6.

of sameness" to be found on both sides of the border.[30] This construction, in all cases, obscures dramatic inequalities.

One of the scholarly theme in narrating life at the border is agency. Mexican women and men are often described as exercising agency when the cross the border into the U.S. for work, medical care or education. But this invites discussion of the moral dilemmas of border crossing, especially those at a border separating a developing nation from a developed nation. Of course one celebrates women who manage, by extraordinary measures, to feed their children adequately. But I found that my study of social relations on the U.S. side of the border increased the complexity of this matter in my thinking. The Imperial County women—all U. S. citizens—are trying to get ahead, trying to achieve the American Dream, defined as a stable job, a home, and decent prospects for their children. Many of them are poor people in a poor place. They experience competition with unauthorized workers as a zero sum game: the number of jobs is limited and every job that goes to someone from "the other side" is one that will not benefit a particular family in their own community. They also fear that their hospital will close and their children's education will suffer. We see that the Imperial County women negotiate multiple macrosystems of inequality that include the local and the global. In U.S. society they experience disadvantage on the basis of their race-ethnicity, social class, gender, and place; however, in respect to relations of inequality in the border region, they are socially privileged. Thus, the paradoxes of life on the border continue.

---

30. Pablo Vila, *Crossing Borders, Reinforcing Borders: Social Categories, Metaphors, and Narrative Identities on the U.S.-Mexico Frontier* (Austin: University of Texas Press, 2000) 124.

Awakening the Desert and Harnessing the Colorado River

Power, Romance, and the Ethics of Water in the Imperial Valley

ALICIA DEWEY

Into the Desert's throat, asleep as dead,
The willful Colorado finds its way;
The Giant wakes, astounded from his dreams,
Imperial Valley's Queen is born today!

> Transformed! The greatest work of God, and one
> Who toiled untiring—honor to his name!
> Thank him, O Queen for your perfected grace
> And bless the hour that your deliverer came.[1]

WATER IS CRUCIAL FOR sustaining life and thus has transformative power, as this 1909 poem about the Colorado River and the Imperial Valley suggests. Judeo-Christian ideals, such as this poem's romantic imagery about turning a desert into a paradise, in addition to democratic values, have shaped water use, law, and policy in the United States throughout its history, although the specific composition and nature of those ideals have changed over time. Power has also directed water allocation; wealthy individuals, private corporations, and even nations have frequently sought to rationalize their efforts to divert water by cloaking impulses of profit and

---

1. Otis B. Tout, "The Desert Awakened . . .," *The Calexico Chronicle: Imperial Valley Second Annual Magazine Edition*, May 1909, 3.

self-interest in the language of justice, generosity, and goodness. Over the last century, conservationists have argued that the needs of the environment must also be considered. The story of the creation of the Imperial Valley of California illustrates how these Judeo-Christian ideals, democratic values, the conservation movement, market forces, and government policies have shaped the development of and discourse about rivers and deserts in the western United States and the U.S.-Mexico borderlands.

The Ecology of the Colorado River and Surrounding Desert

The Colorado River has been called the "river of life" for the dry southwestern corner of the United States. As one of two major rivers in the region (along with the Rio Grande River), it supplies much of the needed water for southern California, Arizona, Utah, New Mexico, Nevada, Utah, and Wyoming. The Colorado River begins as a tiny stream in northeastern Colorado fed by melting snows from Long's Peak that flow down the western slope of the continental divide. As it moves out of the mountains, the stream grows into a powerful river, winding 1,450 miles through mountains, canyons, plateaus, and deserts before it fans out into its delta and struggles to reach the Gulf of California.[2]

Today, the Colorado is the most highly regulated river in the world, with over twenty dams and reservoirs controlling its flow, the ultimate outcome of the desire to reclaim and transform western deserts into hospitable places for settlement. It "has been reduced to a shadow upon the sand, its delta dry and deserted, its flow a toxic trickle seeping into the sea." The river and its surrounding environment looked very different at one time, with a delta that once fanned out into hundreds of streams creating a "vast riparian and tidal wetland the size of the state of Rhode Island . . . one of the largest desert estuaries on earth."[3]

When it was still a wild river, the Colorado picked up and carried millions of tons of fertile silt, dumping it along its banks and pushing it into surrounding valleys, including the low-lying Salton Sink. The Imperial Valley, approximately 100 miles long and thirty-five miles wide, lies in this sink, about 200 feet below sea level. It is surrounded by rugged desert

2. Wade Davis, *River Notes: A Natural and Human History of the Colorado* (Washington, DC: Island, 2013), 14–15.

3. Ibid., 13, 2.

mountain ranges to the west, north, east and southeast and Mexico's Mexicali Valley to the south. One of the mountain ranges separates the Imperial Valley from the Colorado River, making access to fresh water problematic. Annual rainfall averages about three inches. Temperatures in the summer regularly soar to 120 degrees the rainy season usually lasts from December to March with an occasional monsoon occurring in late summer.[4]

Evolving Understandings of Rivers and Deserts

Prior to the late nineteenth century, Spaniards, Mexicans, and Anglo-Americans viewed the land through which the lower Colorado River flowed as a desolate and forbidding place. In the Judeo Christian tradition, deserts represented cursed lands, the "howling wilderness." They symbolized the fallen world marred by sin, places where people went who were cast out of the Garden of Eden. In this tradition, the indigenous people were viewed as pagan and part of this cursed wilderness. In the lower Colorado River valley and delta and surrounding desert areas, they included the Cucapá (or Cocopah), the Kumeyaay or Tipai-Imai, and the Cahuilla, who survived by hunting, fishing, gathering plants such as cactus, agave, mesquite pods, and tule roots, and by planting maize, beans, squash, pumpkins, and watermelons. Spaniard Hernando de Alarcón encountered the Cucapá in 1540 when he was exploring the Gulf of California and reached the mouth of the Colorado. He described them as "tall and strong," "with bodies and faces adorned in paint."[5]

The Judeo-Christian tradition considered the desert wilderness as a place of trial for spiritual growth and strengthening of character. Biblical figures such as Moses, John the Baptist, and the Apostle Paul, and even Christ Himself all spent time in the desert before beginning their ministries. The Book of Exodus recounts the story of the Israelites leaving

---

4. Phillip H. Round, *The Impossible Land: Story and Place in California's Imperial Valley* (Albuquerque: University of New Mexico Press, 2008) 19, 21, 30; Norris Hundley Jr., *Water and the West: The Colorado River Compact and the Politics of Water in the American West* (Berkeley: University of California Press, 1975) 17–18.

5. Davis, *River Notes*, 3–4. The Puritans had a similar conception of the eastern forests and their inhabitants. See, e.g., Increase Mather, *A Brief History of the War with the Indians in New England* originally published in 1676, reprinted in Richard Slotkin and James K. Folsom, eds., *So Dreadfull A Judgment: Puritan Response to King Philip's War, 1676–1677* (Middletown, CT: Wesleyan University Press, 1978) 109–11.

captivity in Egypt to wander in the desert for forty years before entering the Promised Land. Europeans, and later Anglo-Americans, imposed these concepts on the deserts of the American West, which in many ways actually did resemble the Judean wilderness outside of Jerusalem.[6]

In keeping with these traditions, the Spaniards who settled the Colorado River valley were Franciscan friars whose mission was to sacrifice their own comforts in order to convert the pagans of the "wilderness." In 1775, Juan Bautista de Anza pioneered an overland trail through the region from a presidio at Tubac in south central Arizona on his way to founding a settlement at San Francisco. A few years later, in 1780–81, Franciscans accompanied by soldiers followed the Anza Trail to the lower Colorado River valley and founded two missions, Purísima Concepción (near present-day Yuma) and Mission San Pedro y San Pablo de Bicuñer a little farther downriver. The missions were short-lived, however, because the native people resented the intrusion of the Spaniards and their disregard for native rights, lands, and crops. They attacked the missions in July, 1781, killing the padres and destroying buildings and property. The Spaniards never returned, and the Mexicans never attempted to settle the region. Although the Anglo-Americans acquired the territory under the Treaty of Guadalupe Hidalgo after the U.S.-Mexican War ended in 1848, they, too, generally avoided it, considering it part of the larger "Great American Desert," an unredeemable wasteland stretching beyond the Mississippi.[7]

By the mid-nineteenth century, economic growth and population pressures in the eastern United States prompted the federal government to create incentives for development of arid regions of the West. The distribution of western public lands to railroad companies facilitated the growth of a vast railway network that connected places like the Colorado River valley to eastern cities and the national market; a Southern Pacific line reached the area in 1903. The Desert Land Act of 1877 enabled settlers to acquire 640-acre desert tracts (later reduced to 320 acres) at a relatively low cost. This process required the transformation of indigenous lifestyles; in 1876 the federal government created the Torres-Martínez reservation in the Salton Sink for a group of Cahuilla Indians and the Cocopah reservation along the lower Colorado River by executive order of President Woodrow Wilson in

6. Paul T. Nelson, *Wrecks of Human Ambition: A History of Utah's Canyon Country to 1936* (Salt Lake City: University of Utah Press, 2014) 21–22, 27.

7. For a discussion of the Great American Desert, see Henry Nash Smith, *Virgin Land: The American West as Symbol and Myth*, reprint ed. (Cambridge: Harvard University Press, 1970) 174–83.

1917. Reservation Indians moved into the wage labor economy, initially serving as guides and workers on steamboats and later providing labor for the construction of railroads and canals and for commercial agriculture.[8]

Despite these advances, a seemingly insurmountable obstacle remained—the scarcity of water. John Wesley Powell, a one-armed Civil War veteran, college professor, and museum curator, who explored the Colorado and Green Rivers in 1869 and again in 1871, tackled this problem in his *Report on the Lands of the Arid Region of the United States* (1878). Powell argued that watersheds, rather than a formal grid plan as applied in the East, should guide the placement of settlements in the arid West. Inspired by the Hispanic communities of New Mexico and the Mormons of Utah, he proposed organizing small farms into self-governing irrigation districts, which would have the authority to tax and raise bonds to finance waterworks, charge for water usage, and allocate water resources. The flow of streams and tributaries within a particular watershed would determine the boundaries of the districts. Powell rejected development by private enterprise because he believed they would monopolize water resources, thereby potentially depriving some residents of necessary water. He also disliked central planning, instead putting his trust in local citizens.[9]

Powell's theories influenced William Smythe, a promoter, newspaperman and journalist, who became a prominent and vocal advocate for government funding of waterworks to irrigate small farm communities throughout the West. In *The Conquest of Arid America* (1900), Smythe argued that not only did irrigation allow societies to "flourish in the midst of desolate wastes" but also promoted democracy and inhibited land monopoly. He had a romanticized Jeffersonian vision of irrigated family farm communities that would provide a "safety valve" for people seeking to escape overcrowded and impoverished working class neighborhoods in industrialized eastern cities. These irrigated colonies, consisting of small farms of five to ten acres, would produce individual economic autonomy,

---

8. Benny J. Andrés, *Power and Control in the Imperial Valley: Nature, Agribusiness, and Workers on the California Borderland, 1900-1940* (College Station: Texas A & M University Press, 2014) 16–17; Round, *The Impossible Land*, 22–23; Stephen Grace, *Dam Nation: How Water Shaped the West and Will Determine Its Future* (Guilford, CT: Globe Pequot, 2012) 20–21.

9. Donald Worster, *A River Running West: The Life of John Wesley Powell* (Oxford: Oxford University Press, 2001) 115–20; 155–62; 209; 345–70, 440–41; Wallace Earle Stegner, *Beyond the Hundredth Meridian: John Wesley Powell and the Second Opening of the West*, reprint ed. (New York: Penguin, 1992) 366–67; Grace, *Dam Nation*, 24–27.

a rough "social equality," and would further protect against the loneliness of typical rural life. He saw Southern California, including the Imperial Valley as a place of great possibilities and praised the "men of the southern valleys" in "their conquest of desert," comparing them to the "men of the Netherlands" who conquered the sea. Smythe recognized fairly quickly that private capital was insufficient to construct adequate irrigation systems. He played a crucial role in the creation of a federal Reclamation Service, formed in 1902 (renamed the Bureau of Reclamation in 1923), and in the eventual federal takeover of the water works in the Imperial Valley.[10]

While Powell, Smythe, and others worked on the practical aspects of making deserts liveable, literary works began to transform the public's perception of them as barren, ugly, and unredeemable wastelands into places of beauty where people and enterprises could flourish, appealing at times to biblical notions of redemption when describing the transformational power of irrigation. Places like the lower Colorado River valley could become a "Garden of Eden," connoting a reversal of the fall of humans into sin and its curse on the land. A Southern Pacific brochure described "the transformation of this vast, silent, solitary Valley ... the turning of a desert-land into fruitful fields and farms ..." Harold Bell Wright's 1911 novel *The Winning of Barbara Worth* presented a moral vision of the reclamation of the Colorado desert, suggesting throughout that it was ultimately a work of God. Thus, managing rivers and deserts for the purpose of producing food and other staples to meet the needs of people was considered a moral good. Turning deserts into gardens also served a national role by helping to fulfill the nation's "manifest destiny" to spread its civilization across the continent. Some believed, too, that reclaiming deserts would help strengthen the character and moral resolve of U.S. citizens, an idea that meshed with the "strenuous life" movement promoted by President Theodore Roosevelt at the turn of the century.[11] George Wharton James, a pastor turned journalist and photographer, in keeping with the biblical tradition of the wilderness as a place of spiritual formation, wrote after canoeing down the lower Colorado in 1905, "It would be a tremendous

10. William E. Smythe, *The Conquest of Arid America* (New York: Harper, 1900) 43, 46, 51–77, 92, 247–59; Andrés, *Power and Control in the Imperial Valley*, 14.

11. "Imperial Valley, California," Rare Book Collection, Huntington Library (San Francisco: Passenger department, Southern Pacific, 1908) 5; Harold Bell Wright, *The Winning of Barbara Worth* (Chicago: Book Supply, 1911); Round, *The Impossible Land*, 62–63; David W. Teague, *The Southwest in American Literature and Art: The Rise of a Desert Aesthetic* (Tucson: University of Arizona Press, 1997).

pity to reclaim all of the desert . . . It is required for the expansion of the soul, the enlargement of vision of perhaps only a few men, but those men will help influence and benefit the world."[12]

The turn of the century desert aesthetic movement, influenced by nineteenth-century romanticism, also depicted arid landscapes as valuable in their unredeemed state but not because they contributed to character development but simply because they were beautiful, aspects of God's creative handiwork. John Van Dyke's *The Desert* (1901), which launched this movement, was the first published work specifically about the lower Colorado River region. A "kingdom of sun-fire," the Imperial Valley consisted of plains stretching to the "horizon—far as the eye can see—in undulations of gray and gold; ridge upon ridge melts into the blue of the distant sky in lines of lilac and purple; fold upon fold over the mesas the hot air drops its veilings of opal and topaz." He believed that civilization, and hence reclamation, would destroy this beauty. Naturalist and University of Wisconsin professor Aldo Leopold, expressed a similar vision when he described his 1922 canoe trip down the lower Colorado to the sea. The area teemed with cormorants, avocets, willets, widgeons, teal, quail, bobcats, coyotes, raccoons and burro deer. A "verdant wall" of cottonwoods, mesquite, and willow trees divided the river from the dry jagged mountains beyond. During the day, he and his brother reveled in this "milk-and-honey wilderness," and in the evenings, they "sat at peace with the world while the quail sizzled in the Dutch oven, and the sun sank in glory behind the San Pedro Mártir." Leopold never returned to the area after this trip, reasoning, "[i]t is the part of wisdom never to revisit a wilderness, for the more golden the lily, the more certain that someone has gilded it." The writings of Leopold, Van Dyke, and other proponents of the desert aesthetic movement, part of the broader conservation movement championed by John Muir, helped to attract potential settlers to the area in the early twentieth century, influenced the formation of the Imperial Wildlife Refuge in 1941, and led to future carve-outs of protected lands along the river.[13]

---

12. George Wharton James and Carl Eytel, *The Wonders of the Colorado Desert (Southern California): Its Rivers and Its Mountains, Its Canyons and Its Springs, Its Life and Its History, Pictured and Described, Including an Account of a Recent Journey Made Down the Overflow of the Colorado River to the Mysterious Salton Sea* (Boston: Little, Brown, 1906) 353; Andrés, *Power and Control in the Imperial Valley*, 21.

13. John C. Van Dyke, *The Desert: Further Studies in Natural Appearances*, 2nd ed. (New York: Scribner's Sons, 1901); Round, *The Impossible Land*, 37; Aldo Leopold, *A Sand County Almanac* (New York: Oxford University Press, 1966) 151–55; "Imperial

Romanticized visions of the desert's beauty and the power of irrigation to transform it, including its supposed capacity to not only redeem barren lands but also the human soul and to produce a democratic society that fairly allocated water to all who needed it, often shattered as they met the realities of the physical environment and the deeply rooted self-interest of all those who sought to harness the Colorado River. The history of the development of the Imperial Valley reveals this tension between ideals and what was achievable, whether private enterprise or the federal government was involved. Yet all sides used the language of justice and moral righteousness to justify what they sought to accomplish.[14]

Early Development of the Colorado River Valley by Private Capital

The development of the Imperial Valley came in fits and starts. Private capital, beginning with experimental failed ventures and ending with the Southern Pacific Railroad, laid the foundation for the water system. Dr. Oliver Wozencraft, whose path to the gold fields in 1849 took him along a southern route across the lower Colorado River, was the first to envision irrigating the area with gravity canals. He spent the rest of his life unsuccessfully trying to realize his dream. In 1875, Thomas Blythe established a colony less than ninety miles upriver from Fort Yuma and another in Mexico in the Colorado River delta, both of which failed, although the town of Blythe has survived to the present.[15]

Charles R. Rockwood was the first person to plan and promote a successful scheme to introduce irrigated agriculture to the lower Colorado River desert region. Rockwood, an engineer, realized the potential of the

National Wildlife Refuge," U.S. Department of Fish and Wildlife website, https://www.fws.gov/refuge/Imperial/about.html (accessed September 1, 2016).

14. Donald Worster has argued that in reality, elites in the Imperial Valley created a hierarchical society ruled by the few who owned the land and controlled the water rights. Donald Worster, *Rivers of Empire: Water, Aridity, and the Growth of the American West* (New York: Oxford University Press, 1985). Benny Andrés went further and argued that the language of democracy, social equality, and turning the desert into a garden actually disguised the intent of the developers to control and subdue the landscape and create a rigid, racially segregated society based on control of water resources. Andrés, *Power and Control in the Imperial Valley*, 40–41.

15. Norris Hundley Jr., *Dividing the Waters: A Century of Controversy between the United States and Mexico*, 2nd ed. (Berkeley: University of California Press, 1966) 19–20; F. G. Havens, "Our Water Rights," *The Imperial Press* (April 8, 1905) 1.

Salton Sink for irrigated farming while conducting various surveys for railroad and real estate companies as well as the U.S. Geological Survey in the 1880s and 1890s. His Colorado River Land and Irrigation Company failed in the Panic of 1893, so he incorporated the California Development Company ("CDC") in 1896, which successfully began the development of the Imperial Valley.[16]

Rockwood quickly discovered that constructing canals from the Colorado River to the Salton Sink was virtually impossible north of the U.S.-Mexico border because a range of desert hills and mountains west of the river meant that engineers would have to construct a fifteen mile tunnel through the sand hills, the cost of which the company could not afford. Rockwood figured out that he needed to dig a canal in Mexico and divert the water north across relatively flat Mexicali Valley into the low-lying Salton Sink. Rockwood formed a Mexican company, La Socieda de Irrigacion y Terrenos de la Baja California (La Sociedad), in 1898 to purchase 100,000 acres plus a right of way for a canal from Guillermo Andrade, Mexican consul in San Francisco, who owned an enormous tract of land in the Mexicali Valley.[17]

Rockwood hired George Chaffey, an irrigation engineer already well-known for projects in Australia and other parts of Southern California, to design the irrigation system, the centerpiece of which was the Alamo Canal, which traversed fifty miles across Mexican land before turning north and emptying, powered by gravity, into the Salton Sink, renamed "The Imperial Valley" by Chaffey. Finances for the construction of the canals came from $500,000 in bonds from Title Insurance and Trust Company secured by a deed of trust on La Sociedad's land in Mexico. The Imperial Land Company, formed at Chaffey's urging, separated the land sales (which, at least initially, primarily involved facilitating public land filings under the Homestead Act of 1862 and the Desert Land Act of 1877) from water delivery and sales, which were to be handled by thirteen private mutual water companies. Chaffey designed twin border towns, Calexico and Mexicali, to serve as bi-national ports of entry, collecting tariffs and customs duties for each nation. The first water reached the Imperial Valley on June 21, 1901. Between 1901 and 1903, private owners acquired 200,000 acres of public

16. Round, *The Impossible Land*, 53–54.

17. Charles R. Rockwood, "Born in the Desert," *Calexico Chronicle, Imperial Valley Second Annual Magazine Edition* (May, 1909) 12–29; C. C. Tait, "Irrigation in the Imperial Valley, California: Its Problems and Possibilities" (Washington: Government Printing Office, 1908) 12–13.

land. *The Imperial Press* reported, "It is becoming widely known that along this great river is the possibility of creating a region unequaled in America in productive power." By 1905, the population totaled 10,000 people, and 120,000 acres, irrigated by about four hundred miles of canals and laterals, were under cultivation.[18]

A series of challenges beset the project from its inception, and conflicts between the developers and the federal government emerged almost immediately. CDC was undercapitalized and nearly lost its charter for failure to pay a franchise tax. Although the company had perfected its claim under California law to divert water from the Colorado in 1899, both the U.S. and Mexican governments questioned that claim, asserting that the diversion impeded the river's navigability and therefore violated the Treaties of Guadalupe Hidalgo (1848) and Gadsden (1853). A 1901 Department of Agriculture report claimed that most of the soil in the Imperial Valley was too alkaline to grow most crops other than sugar beets, sorghum, and date palms. Then, the Department of the Interior launched an investigation after rumors surfaced that the Imperial Land Company had hired men to file desert homestead claims and then turn the land over to the company so that it could sell the parcels at a profit. This led to the cessation of all land filings and finalization of land claims until 1909, which made it virtually impossible for the settlers in the area to borrow money to develop their farms.[19]

Each side framed the conflict between the private developers and the federal government in moral terms. The federal government emphasized the shady character of the developer-entrepreneurs and accused them of fraud, corruption, and intentional and reckless violation of countless land and water laws. President Theodore Roosevelt charged that the CDC and Imperial Land Company had made "extravagant claims" rising at times to the level of "willful misrepresentation."[20] The Reclamation Service urged

---

18. "Making a New Country," *The Imperial Press* (April 4, 1903) 4; *Title Ins. & Trust Co. v. California Development Co.*, 171 Cal. 173, 152 P. 542 (Ca. Sup. Ct. 1915); Donald J. Pisani, *Water, Land, and Law in the West: The Limits of Public Policy, 1850–1920* (Lawrence: University Press of Kansas, 1996) 229–30.

19. Hundley, *Water and the West*, 22–25; "A Bit of Lower California History in the Life of Guillermo Andrade," *Calexico Chronicle: Imperial Valley Second Annual Magazine Edition* (May 1909) 3; Andrés, *Power and Control in the Imperial Valley*, 29; "The Government's Adverse Soil Report," in L. M. Holt, *The Unfriendly Attitude of the U.S. Government towards the Imperial Valley*, Rare Book Collection, Huntington Library (Imperial: Imperial Daily Standard Print) 11.

20. "Letter from L. M. Holt to the President on Imperial Valley Matters, January 22,

local settlers to abandon the CDC and instead embrace the Yuma storage project (the Laguna Dam system) across the river in Arizona, approved in 1904 and funded under the Newlands Reclamation Act of 1902. William Smythe traveled to the Imperial Valley to urge local farmers to form the Imperial Valley Water Users' Association ("IVWUA"), which held rallies to support government funded irrigation. Smythe assisted the IVWUA in its efforts to negotiate a purchase of CDC's assets for $3 million and form a plan to take over the private mutual water companies.[21]

The private developers, on the other hand, accused the federal government of insincerity, oppression, injustice, and vindictiveness. The activities of the U.S. government had impeded settlement, effectively halted the flow of capital, and endangered the water supply. Local farmers had "struggled along for five years in the faith that someday the government they love would put an end to the persecution they have suffered from branches of the government, which persecution is the primal cause of the trouble the valley has suffered."[22] Anthony Heber, CDC's president, accused Smythe and other leaders of the IVWUA of "anarchistic proclivities." President Theodore Roosevelt became infuriated after some followers of Heber tarred and feathered Paul Van Dimas, one of the IVWUA leaders, and ordered even more investigations into CDC's activities.[23]

Floods between 1905 and 1907 ultimately destroyed the companies created by Rockwood, Heber, and Chaffey, leading to a takeover of the irrigation system by the Southern Pacific Railroad. Substantial snowfall in the Rocky Mountains during the winter of 1905 turned into massive snowmelt that rushed in torrents down the Colorado River toward its delta, contributing to flash floods that gushed through the silt jamming the various intakes built along the river. None had been designed and constructed to control significant flooding. Water poured into the Salton Sink, flooding the New Liverpool Salt Company, inundating Southern Pacific railroad

---

1907," in Holt, *The Unfriendly Attitude of the U.S. Government Towards the Imperial Valley*, 17.

21. Andrés, *Power and Control in the Imperial Valley*, 19.

22. "A Recent Summary by the Imperial Standard, February 8, 1907," in *The Unfriendly Attitude of the U.S. Government towards the Imperial Valley*, 5–6.

23. Anthony H. Heber, "Address of Hon. A. H. Heber, President of the California Development Company, to the Settlers of Imperial Valley: In Support of the Water and Property Rights Owned by the Company in the Valley at Imperial, California, July 25, 1904," Rare Book Collection, Huntington Library (Los Angeles: Southern California, 1904) 39, 54; Andrés, *Power and Control in the Imperial Valley*, 19–21.

tracks, creating the Salton Sea, and threatening the entire irrigation system. Lacking the necessary capital to repair the damage, CDC and La Sociedad filed for receivership. The Southern Pacific stepped in, purchasing the assets of CDC on June 20, 1905, and creating Compania de Terrenos y Aguas de la Baja California ("Compania") to acquire the Mexican water rights of La Sociedad. After floods in 1906 destroyed the railroad's initial repairs to the canals, Edward Harriman, president of the Southern Pacific at the time, was ready to abandon the project. President Theodore Roosevelt became concerned that failure to repair the Imperial Valley diversions might damage the recently constructed federal Yuma project in Arizona. Accusing the Southern Pacific of gross incompetence and reckless disregard, he ordered Harriman to dam the holes in the canals. He held the railroad company, not CDC or its engineers, responsible for the damage. Despite further repair efforts, floods in 1907 surged through and over twenty miles of earthen levees constructed to shore up the river's banks.[24]

The Southern Pacific found itself in the unenviable position of not only having expended enormous sums to repair the irrigation system but also needing to maintain it for the foreseeable future. Not surprisingly, the railroad looked for ways out of its predicament and sought reimbursement from the United States government. From the Southern Pacific's perspective, it had acted altruistically by stepping in, at the request of President Roosevelt, to prevent further disaster to the Laguna Dam, the Yuma project, and the Imperial Valley.[25] The federal government's attitude, at least in some quarters, appeared to soften. Elwood Mead, then Chief of the Irrigation and Drainage Division of the U.S. Department of Agriculture, said that it was actually the federal government's duty to fix the breach that caused the flooding, not the Southern Pacific's, but the U.S. government had shifted responsibility away from itself. Mead noted that Harriman and the Southern Pacific provided "the first refreshing example of generosity and public spirit."[26] The House of Representatives introduced a bill in 1908 to

---

24. *Title Ins. & Trust Co. v. California Development Co.*, 171 Cal. 173, 152 P. 542 (Ca. Sup. Ct. 1915); Andrés, *Power and Control in the Imperial Valley*, 21–26.

25. *Southern Pacific Imperial Valley Claim: Evidence, Statement, and Argument before the Committee on Claims of the House of Representatives on House Bill 9950, Sixty-First Congress, Second Session, to Reimburse the Southern Pacific Company the Amounts Expended by it from December 1, 1906 to November 30, 1907, in Closing and Controlling the Break in the Colorado River*, Rare Book Collection, Huntington Library (Washington, DC: Government Printing Office, 1910) 18.

26. George Kennan, *The Salton Sea: An Account of Harriman's Fight with the Colorado*

compensate the Southern Pacific for the work it had done, and both Presidents Roosevelt and Taft supported the payment. The bill never passed, however, and the Southern Pacific never received any compensation for the $3,000,000 it had paid to fix the damage. It was not until 1916 that the Southern Pacific was able to fully extricate itself from the Imperial Valley water system. It was becoming more and more clear that private capital was insufficient to maintain the irrigation works and allocate adequate water to all who clamored for it.

Mexico and the Imperial Valley

In the midst of escalating hostilities between private entrepreneurs and the U.S. government over the Imperial Valley, more fault lines emerged among Imperial Valley settlers, landowners in the Mexicali Valley, and the government of Mexico. One conflict arose out of a concession that La Sociedad had obtained from the Mexican government after a serious water shortage in 1903–4 threatened to dry up the existing canals. Mexico had allowed the company to divert water through a third intake with the caveat that the Mexicali Valley retained the right to as much as fifty percent of the diverted water. At the time, few people lived in the Mexicali Valley and therefore the threat to the Imperial Valley's water supply was minimal, but this situation would soon change. Harrison Gray Otis, owner and editor of the *Los Angeles Times* and an enormously wealthy businessman, along with his son-in-law Harry Chandler, formed two transnational enterprises, the California-Mexico Land & Cattle Company (1902) and the Colorado River Land Company, to acquire land on both sides of the U.S.-Mexico border. By 1905, the Otis-Chandler interests had purchased approximately 850,000 acres in the Mexicali Valley. The completion of the Inter-California railroad between Mexicali and Yuma in 1909 connected the Mexicali Valley to the transnational railway network, providing much better access to markets, which in turn led to a boom in settlement. It did not help matters that the Southern Pacific and other U.S. entities had spent $8,354,087 for flood protection along the lower Colorado whereas the Mexican government and the Mexicali farmers (including the wealthy Otis-Chandler monopoly) had contributed only $621,908. Imperial Valley farmers saw themselves as fighting exploitative big business. At one point, Anthony Heber even accused Otis' *Los Angeles Times* of crippling

River (New York: Macmillan, 1917) 96.

the farmers, making it impossible for them to get the credit they needed by misrepresenting the nature of the soil and the financial solvency of CDC. The conflict took on racial and nationalistic overtones. Many of the new settlers in the Mexicali Valley were tenant farmers of Asian descent who were finding it increasingly difficult to buy or lease land in California due to intense prejudice. The white, native-born farmers of the Imperial Valley referred to the Asians in derogatory ways, using epithets such as "Japs and Chinamen."[27]

The Mexican Revolution began in 1910, creating even more uncertainty over the reliability of the water supply to the Imperial Valley. One of the first events of the Revolution actually occurred in the Mexicali Valley. Brothers Enrique and Richard Flores Magón, anarchists, syndicalists, supporters of the International Workers of the World, and major thinkers behind the Revolution, hatched a plot while living in exile in Los Angeles to seize the town of Mexicali. Revolutionaries invaded on January 29, 1911, and an insurrection ensued with approximately three hundred Mexicans, Cocopah, white and black unionists, soldiers of fortune, and American deserters joining the revolutionaries. Two hundred Mexican troops failed to oust the *insurrectos*, so the U.S. began to marshal its own troops to protect American lives and property.[28]

The troubles in the Mexicali Valley exacerbated existing views of U.S. citizens that Mexicans were incapable of self-government, unsuited for democracy, and prone to theft. Rumors abounded that tenant farmers on the Otis-Chandler lands were cutting new channels out of the existing canals, thereby weakening them and diminishing the flow to the Imperial Valley. Floating corpses of mules, horses, and human victims of the Revolution contaminated the canals. Although the Revolution did not appreciably disrupt agriculture in either the Mexicali or Imperial Valleys, it raised fears that it would be. Then, the Mexican Constitution of 1917 made it clear that only Mexican citizens and corporations had the right to use water or land;

27. "Acreage of Crops in Valley," *The Imperial Valley Press* (April 18, 1903) 2; "A Bit of Lower California History in the Life of Don Guillermo Andrade," *Calexico Chronicle, Imperial Valley Second Annual Magazine Edition* (May 1909) 34–35; "The California-Mexico Land and Cattle Company," *Calexico Chronicle, Imperial Valley Second Annual Magazine Edition* (May, 1909) 61–62; Hundley, *Water and the West*, 33–34; Andrés, *Power and Control in the Imperial Valley*, 20, 25, 43; Heber, "Address of A. H. Heber," 31.

28. "Big Corporations in America, England, and Germany Want Holdings Protected," *The Salt Lake Tribune* (March 8, 1911) 2; "Largest Force of Armed Men Ever Assembled by Nation in Time of Peace," *Albuquerque Morning Journal* (March 8, 1911) 1; "Asserts Ability to Crush Revolt," *The Evening Star*, Washington, DC, (March 8, 1911) 1.

foreigners were prohibited from owning any land within sixty-two miles of the border, and the federal government could choose to regulate or seize private property at any time in the interests of the public. This put the diversion canals in Mexico at risk. President Álvaro Obregón's appointment of a federal engineer as Chief of First Zone of Irrigation under the Department of Agriculture in 1920, who subsequently launched detailed studies of the hydrology and geography of the region in preparation for the construction of more irrigation works, raised the spectre of even more water use in the Mexicali Valley with new waterworks funded by the Mexican government. Concerned over threats to their water supply, Imperial Valley farmers turned to the federal government for help in building an "All-American Canal" that would obviate the need for Mexico's cooperation in providing water through the Alamo Canal.[29]

Government Takeover

The first steps toward a government takeover of the irrigation system and the construction of an "All-American Canal" occurred in 1911 when the settlers of the Imperial Valley, with the help of lawyer Phil Swing and businessman Mark Rose, formed the Imperial Irrigation District ("IID") under California's 1887 Wright Act. (The Wright Act had originally been designed to give small farmers power over the monopolistic landowners who had been buying up and controlling more and more acreage and hence the water rights.) Notably, the IID, like most other water districts, was not simply comprised of small farmers. One of the largest entities was Harry Chandler's Imperial Valley Farm Lands Association, which had purchased 45,000 acres in 1912 from the Southern Pacific to then sell in small parcels at a profit but had difficulty doing so. The true advantage of these water districts was that they had the power to assess taxes and issue bonds, thereby potentially raising more capital than private enterprise.) Five years after its creation, in 1916, the IID acquired the necessary funds via a $3.5 million bond issue to purchase the irrigation system from the Southern Pacific and build additional flood control measures.[30]

---

29. Andrés, *Power and Control in the Imperial Valley*, 27–31; Hundley, *Water and the West*, 31.

30. Jack L. August, *Dividing Western Waters: Mark Wilmer and Arizona v. California* (Fort Worth: Texas Christian University Press, 2007) 28; Letter from the Governing Board of the Imperial Valley Lands Association signed by Harry Chandler and Luther

The IID's main goal was the construction of the "All-American Canal." Under the direction of Franklin K. Lane, Woodrow Wilson's Secretary of the Interior, the All-American Canal Board consisting of three engineers, including Elwood Mead, conducted a survey in 1918 to evaluate the feasibility of constructing a canal across the East Side Mesa to the Imperial Valley. The study concluded that the project would require digging a sixty-mile tunnel through the sand hills at a cost of about $30 million.[31]

Lacking the ability to raise the necessary capital, the IID sought help from the Reclamation Service and found an ally in Arthur Powell Davis, a civil engineer and the nephew of John Wesley Powell. Davis became the Director of the Reclamation Service in 1914, a role in which he served until 1922. As early as 1902, he had envisioned a series of dams and storage reservoirs along the entire length of the Colorado River and was the first to highlight the need to take an entire watershed into account when planning any kind of irrigation system. He saw the farmers of the Imperial Valley and their need for an "All-American Canal" as natural allies in his effort to build what would be the first of many large dams along the Colorado River. The All-American Canal would be part of his more comprehensive plan for storage and flood control for the entire region.[32]

Davis shared, along with other "irrigation crusaders" including his famous uncle John Wesley Powell, the Jeffersonian vision of creating small, democratically governed farm communities on arid lands in the West. Unlike his uncle, however, he believed that the challenges of supplying water to western communities were so complex and difficult that only the federal government could solve them. As a progressive Republican, he viewed government as an important instrument to achieve political, social and economic goals and believed in the role of expert knowledge to design practical measures for reform. Davis also embraced utilitarian conservation principles championed by President Theodore Roosevelt and Gifford Pinchot, head of the Forestry Service under McKinley, Roosevelt, and Taft, which involved the central management of natural resources so as to maximize their use for the public good and preserve them for future generations.[33]

Brown to the Members of the Imperial Valley Farm Lands Association, November 19, 1915, Rare Book Collection, Huntington Library.

31. August, *Dividing Western Waters*, 29–30; Hundley, *Water and the West*, 37–39.

32. Norris Hundley, *The Great Thirst: Californians and Water, 1770s–1990s* (Berkeley: University of California Press, 1992) 203–4.

33. Ibid.

Davis began pushing for a large dam project above the Imperial Valley along the Arizona-Nevada border in the Boulder Canyon —Black Canyon area. Hiram Johnson, former governor of California, had been elected senator in 1917, and Phil Swing was elected in 1920 to serve in the House of Representatives for the district that included Imperial County and the IID. Johnson and Swing, with the help of Davis and the Reclamation Service, drafted and then introduced the Swing-Johnson Bill (also known as the Boulder Canyon Bill) in 1922. The bill provided for the construction of the dam and an accompanying reservoir, which would be used for three purposes: 1) "river regulation and flood control"; 2) "irrigation and domestic use;" 3) "power." Johnson proclaimed the bill to be "the most ambitious scheme that man lately has conceived. It kindles the enthusiasm and fires the imagination." The dam would be the highest in the world, 600 feet tall, higher than the Washington Monument or any building then in the City of Los Angeles. The reservoir would be one hundred and twenty miles long. Electricity produced by the dam would pay for the cost of construction. The design and funding for the All-American Canal project was included in the overall project.[34]

Not surprisingly, the Chandler companies with extensive holdings in the Mexicali Valley opposed the bill, fearing it would disrupt water to their Mexican lands. In response, Johnson accused them of greed and avarice, "deny[ing] to farmers fighting the desert in America the right to protection, even the right to live" and declared, "we search our memories in vain for a heinous historical parallel of wrong, oppression, and cruelty." Private power companies joined with the Chandler interests and charged the authors of the bill with promoting socialism by creating a vehicle for state-owned hydroelectricity. Johnson faulted the private power companies for "rapacity" and "sordid motives," seeking profit when they were supposed to be providing a public service.[35]

The Boulder Canyon Bill spurred the states that used Colorado River water to negotiate the Colorado River Compact in 1922 regulating each states' use of water. It divided the states into the upper Colorado River basin (Colorado, Wyoming, Utah, and New Mexico) and the lower Colorado River basin (Nevada, California, and Arizona). The Boulder Canyon bill

---

34. Hiram Johnson, *Epic of the Imperial Valley: An Address Delivered before the Commonwealth Club of San Francisco on October 17, 1925 and the Public Spirit Club of Oakland on October 20, 1925*, Rare Book Collection, Huntington Library, 5–7.

35. Ibid., 9–10.

was made contingent upon all seven states ratifying the Compact. The upper basin states ratified the Compact fairly easily once they agreed upon an amount to release to the lower basin. Nevada had little need for water due to its limited population. Arizona, however, long suspicious of California's efforts to dominate the river, refused to ratify. California's reputation as a "lurid and morally corrupt society, with its Hollywood flappers and strange ethnic mixture of Asians and Midwesterners and Italians, of Catholics, Jews, and Protestants . . . a behemoth, the largest and fastest growing state in the basin, and one supremely arrogant" did not help the negotiations. Eventually, the bill's authors changed the language to require only six of the seven states to ratify, and the Boulder Canyon Project Act passed in 1928. The dam, renamed Hoover Dam, was completed in 1936 and the All-American Canal in 1940. Construction of dams along the lower Colorado accelerated thereafter.[36] The IID issued a pamphlet in 1943, shortly after the completion of the projects that declared:

> The history of the Imperial Valley is a dramatic tale of a struggle against drought and inundation, against a silt laden water whose huge deposits choked up canals and drains, against control by a foreign country of the Valley's life blood, its water supply. The construction of Boulder Dam and of the All-American Canal . . . has provided a final solution to these problems.[37]

Seemingly, the transformation of the Imperial Valley from a desert into a garden was complete with a constant water supply assured for the foreseeable future. Yet, rather than a democratic community of small farmers, by the mid-twentieth century, government-managed irrigation (along with other market forces and technological developments) had created an agricultural society in the Imperial Valley "characterized by highly commercialized, large scale operations," according to a 1943 pamphlet produced by the IID. Absentee owners controlled half of the land, which was farmed by "Mexicans, Orientals, negroes, and migrant whites under the direction of white foremen."[38] The romantic image of the hardy settler, struggling against the challenges of an arid environment and seeking community with like-minded individuals, had disappeared into the mists of time, to be re-

---

36. Hundley, *Water and the West*, 211–14. Hundley's entire book goes into detail about how the Colorado River Compact was negotiated and ratified.

37. Charles P. Burgess, "Imperial Irrigation District," Rare Book Collection, Huntington Library (San Francisco: Kaiser, 1943) foreword.

38. Burgess, "Imperial Irrigation District," 2–4.

placed by "factories in the field," in the words of Carey McWilliams. As one writer put it, "The rude tent-house, the arrow-weed ramada, the rough board shack, the fire and bed under the mesquite, and the shelter less camp on the desert sands have passed into the keeping of the historian and novelist. . . .The hardy, dust-grimed, mud-caked, sunburned reclaimer of the desert no longer makes his lonely fire and with his own rude hand prepares the bacon, frijoles, flapjacks and coffee for his solitary meal."[39]

In U.S. society today, few people evaluate how reclamation or desert experiences might form character or how the distribution of water resources might promote democracy. Instead, social justice principles, which incorporate Judeo-Christian ethics of sharing and meeting human needs, strongly influence how U.S. and world leaders allocate water. Many see access to clean water as a human right and the conservation of water a responsibility of all. The story of the lower Colorado River and the Imperial Valley raises the question of who is best positioned to protect water resources and provide access to them most equitably. Did the U.S. government achieve justice when it stepped in to take over from the private entrepreneurs? Many thought not, especially residents of Mexico and Arizona. Mexico, in particular, believed that it had been robbed of its water and used the Colorado as leverage in negotiating the 1944 Treaty with Mexico relating to the Utilization of the Waters of Certain Rivers, which had been spurred by the needs of farmers in the Lower Rio Grande Valley for water from Mexican rivers that fed the Rio Grande. Despite promises made in that treaty, Mexico receives very little water from Colorado today because the river has been over-allocated to upstream users. The more wealthy and powerful agricultural, business, and government interests seem to have the capacity to exert control over water in such a way that they achieve what they want. Environmental activists seem to provide the most persistent moral voice against further irrigation, often to the detriment of economic growth. They push for curtailing agricultural activities and some even support the removal of dams, which have altered the riverine environment and created problems for native plants and wildlife. As water resources become scarcer, we will be increasingly confronted with the moral challenge of articulating and applying an inclusive ethic of water that considers the needs

---

39. *Imperial Valley, 1901–1915*, Rare Book Collection, Huntington Library (Los Angeles: Kingsley, Mason, & Collins, 1915); Carey McWilliams, *Factories in the Field: the Story of Migratory Farm Labor in California*, rev. ed. (Berkeley: University of California Press, 2000).

of productive enterprise as well as those of individual people and communities in all parts of the world.[40]

40. Christopher Meehan, "The Ethics of Water," *Homiletic and Pastoral Review*, October 22, 2013, http://www.hprweb.com/2013/10/the-ethics-of-water/ (accessed July 5, 2016); Committee on Foreign Relations, "Treaty with Mexico Relating to the Utilization of the Waters of Certain Rivers," ed. U.S. Senate (Washington, DC: Government Printing Office, 1944); Andrés, *Power and Control in the Imperial Valley*, 96; "The Salton Sea: the Environmental and Economic Values of this Vast Inland Lake Prompt Local Officials to Launch a New Restoration Effort," Western Waters, Water Education Foundation, March/April 1994, 3–11, http://www.sci.sdsu.edu/salton/EnvirnEconValueSaltonSea.html (accessed September 13, 2016).

Richard Henry Dana Jr., Evangelical Consciousness, and the Colony of Hawaiians in San Diego

Rick Kennedy

In the first chapter of the first book of Kevin Starr's magisterial series *Americans and the California Dream*, Richard Henry Dana Jr.'s *Two Years Before the Mast* is offered as an example of a "prophetic pattern" of "Protestant consciousness." The book and Dana's own life are presented as presaging California's cultural struggle with a Protestantism that is wrapped up in the self, conflicted by sex, myopically industrious, and overly judgmental. Dana's book and Dana himself, for Starr, embed a Protestant consciousness in California when the place was at the "beginnings of becoming the cutting edge of the American Dream."[1]

That Kevin Starr would give such cultural significance to the mentality of one young man and his book might seem to be a wild assertion, but it is not without merit. *Two Years Before the Mast* was immediately popular, widely read for many years, and when Dana revisited California after the Gold Rush, he was astonished to find that he was held in outsized esteem. "When California 'broke out,' as they phrase it, in 1848," Dana later wrote, "and so large a portion of the Anglo-Saxon race flocked to it, there was no book upon California but mine."[2] In 1859, when revisiting California, Dana found himself a cultural hero in a fast-growing state looking to es-

---

1. Kevin Starr, *Americans and the California Dream* (New York: Oxford, 1973) 46; the analysis of Dana runs from 38–48.

2. Richard Henry Dana Jr., "Appendix: 'Twenty-four Years After,'" in *Two Years Before the Mast: A Personal Narrative of Life at Sea*, introduced by Gary Kinder (New York: Modern Library Paperback, 2001) 416.

tablish and promote a new Anglo-Saxon and Protestant identity. On that visit Dana noted in his journal: "State pride of Californians very strong. Remote. Severed by Ocean & Rocky Mountains fr. rest of world, & have peculiar climate, & peculiar habits & history."[3] While revisiting California, Dana realized that he and his book had become very important to the new state's pride and sense of identity.

Because Kevin Starr has it arguably right that Dana and his book have a prophetic role in the formation of California's religious culture, it is important that we get that role correct. When Starr focuses on the way Dana personally escaped "suffocating orthodoxies" by coming to California, he misses the most distinctive religious perspective evident in the book and in Dana's life.[4] *Two Years Before the Mast* was written out of an evangelical consciousness that historian Charles Foster has called *An Errand of Mercy: The Evangelical United Front 1790–1837*.[5] In that important and wide-ranging book, Foster probably overstates the unitedness of what was more just an entangled fellowship of optimistic evangelicals, but much of Dana's book and his life as sailor and young author is best understood as a minor Boston-California offshoot within the larger story of British and American hopes to bring evangelical uplift to the globe—especially to what is today called the "Pacific World." The hope was grand and Dana presents himself only doing his small bit among a "colony" of twelve to twenty Hawaiians on a little Mexican beach, *La Playa* on Point Loma, three miles south of the village of San Diego.[6] Dana's small bit for the cause soon reverberated into California's cultural beginnings through the popularity of *Two Years Before the Mast*. Here in this essay, I will first show the important role of Hawaiians in *Two Year Before the Mast*, then show how Dana's life had already been part of an Evangelical-Hawaiian alliance in New England, and end with the evangelical factors that helped facilitate the writing of *Two Years Before the Mast*. Recognizing that Starr's *America and the California Dream* has, itself, become a classic of California literature, I hope to make stronger and

---

3. Richard Henry Dana Jr., *The Journal of Richard Henry Dana, Jr.*, ed. Robert F. Lucid (Cambridge: Harvard University Press, 1968) 3:908.

4. Starr, *Americans and the California Dream*, 38.

5. Charles I. Foster, *An Errand of Mercy: The Evangelical United Front, 1790–1837* (Chapel Hill: University of North Carolina Press, 1960).

6. Richard Henry Dana Jr., *Two Years before the Mast: A Personal Narrative of Life at Sea*, intro. Gary Kinder (New York: Modern Library Paperback, 2001) chap. 19, p. 158. All citations of page numbers are from this edition. Because there are many popular editions, chapter numbers are cited.

more specific Starr's description of *Two Years Before the Mast* as "a work of imaginative reconnaissance" for California.[7]

Dana's appreciation of Hawaiians appears throughout the California-coast section of *Two Years Before the Mast*, and he wants his readers to develop a deep love for them too. On his first encounter with the coast in January 1835 he tells a vivid and appreciative story of learning from Hawaiians how to surf a rowboat to shore. When he leaves California in May 1836, three Hawaiian friends walk with him down to the shore. As Dana rows back to his ship, the Hawaiians walk away "chanting one of their deep monotonous songs the burden of which I gathered to be about us and our voyage."[8] The night before sailing, Dana wrote that he was with "my Kanaka friends." Desperately anxious to return to Boston, Dana says that leaving the Hawaiians was "the only thing connected with leaving California which was in any way unpleasant."[9]

Although Dana encountered Hawaiians at every anchorage in California, his book focuses on their shared life at the Hawaiian "colony" at *La Playa* on Point Loma. *La Playa* was a beach community at the main anchorage in San Diego Bay. Ships sailing north into the lee of *La Punta de la Loma* passed by a small Mexican fort on a low spit of sand and gravel called Ballast Point (*Punta de los Guijarros*), then anchored near *La Playa*. With no surf with which to contend, somewhat protected from the prevailing winds, isolated from the presidio-town where the ship captains would stay, Dana found happiness at *La Playa*. Santa Barbara's surf was a struggle, San Pedro depressed him, and the anchorage for San Juan Capistrano (now named Dana Point) was risky. In one of the book's most poignant moments, Dana in Santa Barbara depicts himself "in a little vessel, with a small crew, on a half-civilized coast, at the ends of the earth."[10] In the San Diego passages of the book, Dana's struggle, despair, and anxiety are gone. Dana describes *La Playa* as "a snug little place, and seeming quite like home."[11]

Dana lived at *La Playa* for two extended periods totaling six months: May 8 to September 8, 1835 and early March to May 8, 1836. In the book, these months are described as happy times: workers are allowed to work without pressure, productivity is high along with morale, and evenings are

7. Starr, *Americans and the California Dream*, xiii.
8. Dana Jr., *Two Years*, 29:297. See ibid., 9:64–65, for the first encounter.
9. Ibid., 29:297.
10. Ibid., 14:101.
11. Ibid., 28:265.

full of multi-ethnic, multi-lingual, and multi-national comradery. Dana depicts life on Point Loma in 1835–36 as a type of Jacksonian worker-paradise.[12] Sharing the beach were twenty Italians, more than a dozen Hawaiians, a dozen Mexicans, varying numbers of Englishmen, Yankees, Scotchmen, Welshmen, Frenchmen, Spaniards, Chileans, and "one Negro, one Mulatto . . . one Otaheitan, and one Kanaka from the Marquesas Islands."[13] Pan-tribal Indians also worked the port and shared in the life of *La Playa*.[14] Unlike the other residents of *La Playa*, the Hawaiians did not sign contracts attaching them to a ship and placing them under the command of a captain. Hawaiians negotiated their labor job by job. Dana noted that they were therefore free to come and go as they pleased, and happily worked only when they wanted and with whom they wanted.[15]

Not being bound to a ship, they were not bound to camp and sleep at any of the two-story hide barns built and owned by shipping companies. The Hawaiians were free to separate themselves into a "colony." This they did at a "Russian oven" that came to be called the "Kanaka Hotel" or "Oahu Coffee-house."[16] Dana writes that a few years before his arrival at Point Loma a Russian ship's crew had built a large oven on the high ground above the beach in which to bake a large quantity of bread, apparently in preparation for a long cruise. After the Russians had sailed away, the oven was large

---

12. Recent scholarship has often tended treat Dana harshly and to emphasize his Yankee form of racism, nationalism, and class consciousness. See, for example, Brett Garcia Myhren, "Consider the Ravens: Indolence and Imperialism in California," in *Southern California Quarterly* 97 (2015) 136–53. In this essay I do not deny these aspects of Dana's perspective. I merely emphasize the humanitarian and good-hearted side of Dana that is evident especially when he is living in the community on Point Loma. I attribute these good qualities to Dana's Jacksonian idealism that runs contrary to his class and to Evangelical consciousness derived from a particular experience with Andover Evangelicals.

13. Dana Jr., *Two Years*, 20:173.

14. For several hundred years before the arrival of the Spanish, the Ipai Indians, the northern division of Kumeyaay, had an encampment, possibly a year-round settlement, at *La Playa*. It is likely they still had a settlement on Point Loma on the trail between the port and the village. Although in the book, Dana depicts no Indians living on *La Playa* in the middle 1830s, he mentions Indians coming and going along with this pleasant description: "The Indians who always have a holyday on Sunday, were engaged in playing a kind of running ball game . . . Some of the girls ran like greyhounds" (ibid., 16:130). Indian girls also resided temporarily among the men on *La Playa*. A shipmate, after publication of the book, chided Dana for not mentioning "the *beautiful Indian Lasses*, who so often frequented your humble abode in the *hide house* . . ." Dana Jr., *Journal*, 1:28n45.

15. Dana Jr., *Two Years*, 18:153–54.

16. Ibid., 19:166.

enough to sleep six to eight people. This oven apparently looked like an adobe igloo. One entered through a low door, and there was a hole in the top. By the time Dana arrived, the oven had already become "headquarters" for the colony of Hawaiians on the coast of California. When Dana returned to California in 1859 he looked for the Kanaka Hotel but found only a few bricks. The Hawaiians were gone.[17]

17. Dana Jr., *Journal*, 3:848. See "Historic Landmarks of San Diego County," *San Diego Historical Society Quarterly* 14 (1968) 61 (http://www.sandiegohistory.org/journal/68july/index.htm). For the history of the site of the "hide houses" and "Russian oven," see Ronald V. May, "The United States Quarantine Station on Point Loma (1893–1937) and Its Place in the History of La Playa," *Fort Guijarros Quarterly* 2 (1988) 10–17 (http://soap.sdsu.edu/FortGuijarros/1988Vol2No4/FortGuijarrosVol2No4.pdf). In an email to Rick Kennedy (Feb. 25, 2016), Ronald V. May, who served for thirty-two years as director of archaeology programs and chairman of the board of directors of the Fort Guijarros Museum Foundation, wrote: "To my knowledge, construction of Navy facilities just inside the entrance to Naval Base Point Loma destroyed most of the historical La Playa archaeology. The existing multi story office building is deeply embedded in the old landform and the surrounding parking lots were dug deep as well. One utility trench cut by Navy Public Works staff exposed portions of a Trade Porcelain charger from the 1840s, which suggested some of the historical archaeology context might remain intact. But the chances for finding the Russian oven seem remote at best. Several historical archaeologists over the years attempted to obtain permission from the Navy to inspect the grounds, but were denied due to the classified nature of what the Navy is doing out there."

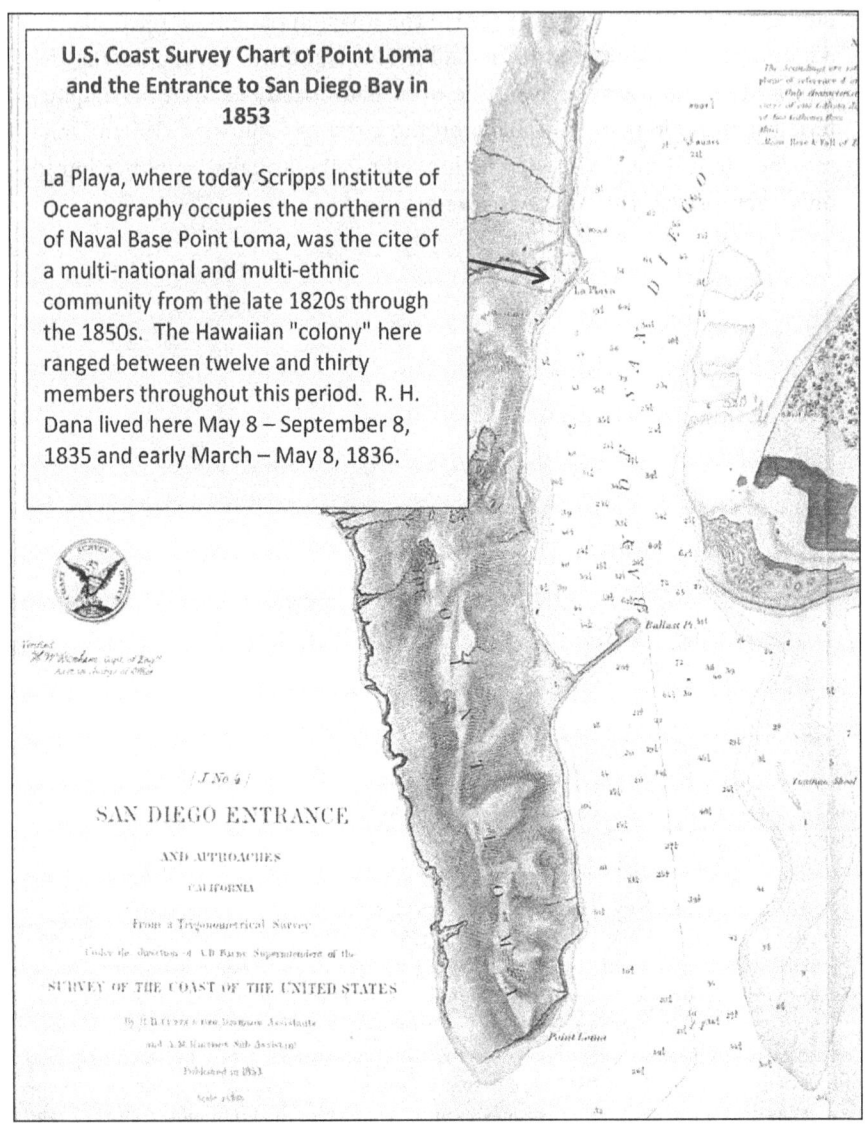

> U.S. Coast Survey Chart of Point Loma and the Entrance to San Diego Bay in 1853
>
> La Playa, where today Scripps Institute of Oceanography occupies the northern end of Naval Base Point Loma, was the cite of a multi-national and multi-ethnic community from the late 1820s through the 1850s. The Hawaiian "colony" here ranged between twelve and thirty members throughout this period. R. H. Dana lived here May 8 – September 8, 1835 and early March – May 8, 1836.

1853 Coast Survey Chart of Point Loma, La Playa, and the Entrance to San Diego Bay. Courtesy of the Central Library of the National Oceanic and Atmospheric Administration (NOAA).

The appreciation of Hawaiians in the *Two Years Before the Mast* is first founded on their boating skills but becomes based in their collective culture and individual characters. Their boating skills were obvious. At the first encounter in Santa Barbara the Bostonians were taken aback by the heavy surf and sat in their rowboat wondering how to get into the beach when the "dusky Sandwich Islanders" working for a newly arrived Italian ship, showed them how to give a shout, pull hard on the oars, catch the top of a wave, throw the oars wide from the boat as it raced forward in the froth, leap out, and run the boat up onto the sand.[18] "They are complete water-dogs," he writes, "and therefore very good in boating. It is for this reason that there are so many of them on the coast of California; they being very good hands in the surf. They are also quick and active in the rigging."[19] Dana enjoys reporting their activities, such as a group in shallow water trying to wrestle a large shark to shore, and another story of a swimmer who chases down a boat leaving San Diego. The swimmer reaches the boat, the captain receives his message, gives him a shot of brandy, and sends him back over the side to swim to shore. Dana writes: "I certainly never saw such swimming before."[20]

But Dana does not dwell only on Hawaiian water skills. Early in the book, on his first trip to Monterey, he rows over to visit the Italian *Loriotte* and "became very well acquainted with her Sandwich Island crew." He describes their "intelligent countenances," and though initially put off by the guttural sound of their language, he notes that "it improves as you hear it more." Adding a note from something he learned in New England, he writes that the Hawaiian language "is said to have great capacity."[21] In San Diego, Dana is entranced by the singing of a Hawaiian named Mahanna. "This fellow had a very peculiar, wild sort of note, breaking occasionally into a falsetto. The sailors thought that it was too high, and not enough of the boatswain hoarseness about it; but to me it had a great charm."[22]

In *Two Years before the Mast* Dana enjoys a reputation as a linguist, and Dana reports that he learned the "mixed language [that the Hawaiians] used on the beach."[23] In his book he transcribes various conversations in this pidgin Hawaiian. He admits, though, that he cannot

---

18. Dana Jr., *Two Years*, 9:64–67.
19. Ibid., 13:93.
20. Ibid., 20:180, 22:189–90.
21. Ibid., 13:93.
22. Ibid., 17:136.
23. Ibid., 19:158–59. For a discussion of Dana and Hawaiian language, see Emanuel J. Drechsel, *Language Contact in the Early Colonial Pacific: Maritime Polynesian Pidgin before Pidgin English* (Cambridge: Cambridge University Press, 2014) 190–93.

understand the songs the Hawaiians sing. "I never could detect a word I knew," Dana writes, but he believes that in the songs the Kanakas were often having fun at the expense of the Americans and Englishmen. While working side by side with singing Kanakas he notes that they would occasionally break into shouts and laughter. Some of the Hawaiians were quick to improvise songs about *Haole* workers. "They have great powers of ridicule, and are excellent mimics."[24]

Dana tells us that at *La Playa* he worked side-by-side with, and became friends with, four Hawaiians. Each had a Hawaiian name, but each also had a working name. "Mr. Bingham" took the name of the first New England missionary to Hawaii. "Hope" took the name of a vessel in which he had served.[25] "Pelican" got his name from "his fancied resemblance to that bird." And "Tom Davis" took the name of a former ship captain. Tom Davis spoke English well, could do mathematics, had been in Nantucket, and had "an education as good as that of three quarters of the Yankees in California."[26] From Mr. Bingham Dana learned much about the history of Hawaii. Of the four, Hope was his favorite: "I really felt strong affection for him, and preferred him to any of my own countrymen."[27] To these four Dana took upon himself the role of teacher, showing and explaining maps and using pictures in old newspapers to expand their knowledge of the whole world. All four were "astonishingly quick in catching at explanations ... they often seized in an instant, and asked questions which showed that they knew enough to wish to go further."[28] Hope was especially interested in learning to read, and Dana taught him letters and numbers. Hope was especially curious to hear about "Boston"—Dana notes that that is what they call the whole United States. As for Hawaiians, Dana writes, they call themselves *Kanaka* and white people *Haole*. Dana notes that Hope calls him *Aikane* which means a special friend. Later in October, Dana describes all the Hawaiians on Point Loma calling him *Aikane*.[29]

---

24. Ibid., 19:163.

25. Samuel E. Morison noted that a ship named *Hope*, from Boston, was in Hawaii in May 1792. See "Boston Traders in Hawaiian Islands, 1789–1823," in *Washington Historical Quarterly*, 12 (1921) 168 (https://journals.lib.washington.edu/index.php/WHQ/article/viewFile/6191/5265).

26. Dana Jr., *Two Years*, 19:158–62.

27. Ibid., 28:266.

28. Ibid., 19:161.

29. Ibid., 19:158, 161, 24:216.

Hope became sick, and for a while looked as though he was going to die. In the book Dana takes this opportunity to note that the European discovery of the Pacific Islands was a "curse." Commerce with white men had brought vices and diseases. The Pacific Islanders "seem to be a doomed people. The curse of a people calling themselves Christian, seems to follow them everywhere."[30] On the other hand, Dana was there to care for him, especially to find medicine for him. Dana gets himself in trouble with one captain for giving medicine to Hawaiians, but the other two captains that Dana deals with are willing to share. One, Captain Arthur, knows Hope, is fond of him, and personally brings to him proper medicines. Dana goes to see Hope the night before he is to leave California, and Hope is responding to the medicine. Hope shakes Dana's hand and says he soon will be well again. Hope tells Dana that he will gladly work for him when Dana returns to California as an officer of his own ship.

These are Dana's last recorded moments on shore in California: He shakes Hope's hand. Three Hawaiians help him shove off from shore in order for him to row out to the ship. The three Hawaiians turn and walk back up to the oven "chanting one of their deep monotonous songs the burden of which I gathered to be about us and our voyage."[31] It is a powerful passage with a message: White men in the Pacific may be a curse, but the work of the curse can be broken. What Pacific-people need is for white men like Dana and Captain Arthur to come with their medicine, their education, their good hearts, their offer of civilization, and, by implication, their offer of salvation. In an earlier passage, Mr. Bingham, "a sort of patriarch" among the Hawaiians, praised the missionaries who had come to Hawaii and changed the customs of his boyhood. Dana then tells his readers: "Certainly the history of no people on the globe can show anything like so rapid an advance."[32] In *Two Years Before the Mast* what had happened in Hawaii was being writ small on the little beach on Point Loma. To evangelical-minded readers in the middle of the nineteenth century the message would have been clear: Those who will come to California in good will and good faith will be welcomed as *aikane* and can help serve in the progress of a friendship-based civilization in California and the Pacific.[33]

30. Ibid., 28:265.
31. Ibid., 29:297. See 9:64–65 for the first encounter.
32. Ibid., 19:160.
33. William R. Hutchinson in *Errand into the World: American Protestant Thought and Foreign Missions* (Chicago: University of Chicago Press, 1987) offers a critical view

California Dreaming

As Kevin Starr notes, the book *Two Years Before the Mast* is an imaginative retelling of events. There is no reason to doubt his narrative about life with Hawaiians on Point Loma; however, it is reasonable to assume that Dana crafted his narrative out of evangelical concerns that were heavy on his mind in the four years before the voyage, the two years during the voyage, and the two years after the voyage including the year, 1838, when he finished the manuscript of his text. As Starr recognizes, to understand the appeal of the book, what happened to Dana in Massachusetts is as important as what happened to Dana in California.

In an autobiographical sketch written in 1841, Dana wrote that the most significant aspect of the years 1830–1838 was not his voyage to California, but rather his turn away from the mild Unitarianism and Congregationalism of his friends and family to what he called an "evangelical" view of Christianity.[34]

As Dana tells it, when he was fifteen years old in 1830, the year before he entered Harvard, he suffered from "depressions" and "spiritual warfare." He had been "religiously taught, but very early gave up prayer & estranged myself entirely from God."[35] At fifteen years old, he was moved to "deep religious convictions" by his dynamic pastor, the Rev. Nehemiah Adams, a great antagonist to theological liberalism. At this time began his conversion, but it took eight years to complete. When late in 1832, during his freshman year at Harvard, he was suspended for six months due to principled non-compliance with an unreasonable administration (Dana's father supported his non-compliance), the spiritually troubled young man was sent to study and live with an evangelical family in Andover. What gets missed in biographies of Dana is that he was exiled from spiritually sleepy and navel-gazing Harvard into the Woods family, a household at the center of the development of the American evangelical vision of what we today call Global Christianity. All biographies of Dana note the influence of Leonard Woods Jr. who was his twenty-four-year-old tutor, and they recognize the importance of Leonard's young sister. They sometimes mention the mother,

---

of the role of missionaries in the Pacific and notes the influence of Herman Melville's criticisms in the novels *Typee* (1846) and *Omoo* (1847). Hutchinson (and Melville) do note attempts, like Dana's, but not mentioning Dana, to distinguish destructive "civilizing" from more focused benevolent missionary methods. On this more careful method, Hutchinson emphasizes the work of Rufus Anderson, a student of Leonard Woods Sr. at Andover Theological School. See Hutchinson's chapter "Christ, Not Culture," 62–90.

34. Dana, *Journal*, 1:32. The account of his conversion runs from 30–35.
35. Ibid.

but biographies of Dana do not recognize the father's role in Dana's life.[36] We can best understand Dana's emphasis on Hawaiians in California if we remember that Dana sat at the dinner table for six months with Leonard Woods Sr. (1774–1854), one of the most dynamic evangelical, mission-minded, intellectuals of the early American republic.

But first we should look to the son. Leonard Woods Jr. (1807–1878) was Dana's young tutor who later became president of Bowdoin College. He appears often in Dana's *Journal* and was much praised by Dana in a eulogy. From this tutor, eight years older than Dana, we can see the roots of some of the most interesting passages in *Two Years Before the Mast*: the interest in Roman Catholic missions and ceremony, especially the funeral and wedding in Santa Barbara, the pietistic concern for Sabbath-breaking, Bible-reading, and temperance, and finally the travelers sense of delight "in the beautiful and the good, the strange and the ancient, and hospitably entertaining whatever is worthy and true."[37]

Leonard Woods Jr. was deep in a scholarly project when the sixteen years old Dana came to join the household. Because of his own project, he gave Dana a lot of unstructured time to pursue wide reading and study. Also in the house was Leonard's fourteen years old sister, Sarah, who became infatuated with Dana. Dana apparently shared with her his struggles with melancholia and his fears that his new found evangelical faith was not as strong as it should be. Sarah, being spiritually precocious, took upon herself the project of helping Dana. Even after he left the household and sailed to California, she continued to pray for him.

When Dana returned to Boston in September 1836 and reconnected with the Woods family, he discovered that the now eighteen-year-old Sarah had just died. Sarah's mother told Dana that in the delirium before her death, Sarah had spoken his name. The mother said that in a later period of lucidness she had asked Sarah why she had called out Dana's name.

---

36. See footnote 46 for biographies of Dana.

37. See Dana's eulogy "Leonard Woods" in *Scribner's Monthly Magazine* (November 1880): 138–144, quote from p. 143, *https://www.unz.org/Pub/Century-1880nov-00138a02* (accessed January 2016). For comparison with Dana's fascination with Catholic ceremony and his light-hearted comparison between the work ethic of Catholicism with New England Protestantism, read the extremely harsh statement that "Catholicism as developed both in Spanish N & S Americas is hardly a better handmaid of Civilization or of humanity than Paganism itself," by New Englander and "liberal interpreter of the Bible," Chester S. Lyman in *Around the Horn to the Sandwich Islands and California 1845–1850*, ed. Frederick J. Teggart (Freeport, NY: Books for Libraries, 1971, first published in 1924), 35 and xvii.

Sarah responded that she had long been praying for him. Dana recorded in his journal that Sarah, knowing that she would die soon, told her mother that she hoped that God, when she was in heaven, would permit her to "watch over me, keeping me from sin, & influencing me toward God & holy things." Dana further recorded that "in her very last moments she prayed fervently & impassionedly for me, & the last words that fell from her lips were 'Prepare him for a seat at thy right hand.'"[38]

Deeply moved by this, having just returned from his trip to California, Dana recommitted himself to his pre-voyage evangelical aspirations. The following year, 1837, became an intense time of finding himself spiritually and vocationally. Fully committed now to an evangelical path, he graduated from Harvard, entered law school, and, in 1838, during a six-month stretch, he wrote almost all of *Two Years Before the Mast*.[39]

Sarah, Leonard Jr., and their mother are all mentioned in Dana's writings, but the clearest connection with evangelical missions to the Pacific was through the unnamed head of the household, Leonard Woods Sr. This older Woods had graduated from Harvard in 1796 and was a leader among intellectuals who thought that Harvard was a bastion of blandness. In 1808 he became one of the founding faculty and first professor of theology at Andover Theological Seminary, an institution founded in opposition to Harvard. Two years later he was one of the founders of the American Board of Commissioners for Foreign Missions. Andover, both seminary and town, became a hot-bed of missionary thought for the next several decades. In 1812, Woods Sr. published a sermon that he had preached at the ordination of missionaries to Asia. In that sermon, writes Margaret Bendroth, "Woods laid out, really for the first time, a theological rationale for global Christianity." Bendroth goes on to note that Woods Sr. saw missionaries as doing more than just conversion, they were to be "a labor of 'love for souls.'" Missionaries were supposed to be broadly interested in a foreign nation's "climate, color, language, government, education, manners." Woods demanded that missionaries be lovers of all: "Learned and ignorant, refined and rude, honorable and base, are all on a level in point of accountableness to God and immortality of soul."[40] Woods Sr., himself, was a broad thinker who saw the evangelization of the globe in multi-dimensional terms. He

---

38. Dana Jr., *Journal*, 1:33.

39. Ibid., 1:xxxv–xxxvi.

40. Margaret Lamberts Bendroth, *A School of the Church: Andover Newton across the Centuries* (Grand Rapids: Eerdmans, 2008) 53.

was one of the founders of the American Tract Society (New England), The American Education Society, the American Temperance Society, and the Association for Better Observance of the Sabbath. He also promoted the work of the American Bible Society and the American Sunday School Union. As Foster shows in *An Errand of Mercy: The Evangelical United Front*, Leonard Woods Sr., along with his family, friends, neighbors, colleagues, and students, were working to make Andover a model community of piety and benevolence that thought and acted both locally and globally.[41] The world would benefit because Andover existed.

Into this high thinking household and community came young Dana to live for six months. Fresh from his evangelical conversion experience he was ready to be devoted to his smart young tutor, ready to discuss his religious struggles with his tutor's little sister, and excited to be part of a lively household watched over by a loving mother and vigorous father—Dana's own mother had died when he was seven years old, and his father, Richard Henry Dana Sr., was widely believed to be indolent and unfulfilled as a poet.[42] While Dana was in Andover, Leonard Woods Sr. was collecting letters from missionaries that he would publish the following year in *Memoirs of American Missionaries, Formally Connected with the Society of Inquiry, Respecting Missions in the Andover Theological Seminary*. Woods Sr. had been a founder of this "Society of Inquiry," a sort-of college club that recruited young men to consider missionary work. The letters he collected and published were all from former students of his, graduates of Andover, who were now all over the world. His introduction to the collection declared his continuing goal to "cultivate the *spirit* of Missions" among students at Andover and in New England. He wanted his book to give examples of where "much is done to promote *the Spirit* of *Christian-benevolence and piety among the mass of the people*."[43] It is hard to imagine that Professor Woods, sitting at his dinner table with young Dana, did not encourage the young man to think about traveling the high seas to far off places where he could do good. When Dana eventually left the Woods home, he found himself un-

---

41. Foster, *An Errand of Mercy*, 134–35.

42. Dana's mother, Ruth Charlotte (Smith) Dana, a former school-teacher, was frail and died in 1822, probably of tuberculosis.

43. Leonard Woods, "Introductory Essay," *Memoirs of American Missionaries, Formally Connected with the Society of Inquiry, Respecting Missions in the Andover Theological Seminary* (Boston: 1833) vii, ix. The book includes a letter from Hiram Bingham and Asa Thurston in Hawaii. Accessed at https://ia700408.us.archive.org/16/items/memoirsofamerica00soci/memoirsofamerica00soci.pdf.

happy back at Harvard. Soon he found a reason to go to California, that isolated coast on the far side of the world. Sad to say, Dana did not show in California as much *Christian-benevolence* as he might. Dana had trouble appreciating various aspects of Mexican and Indian culture; however, the Woods household had well-prepared him to appreciate Hawaiians.

Andover had been introduced to Hawaiians in 1810 by Henry Opukaha'ia (spelled Obookiah by New Englanders of his day).[44] Opukaha'ia became an exotic celebrity throughout New England. Sixteen years old, barely speaking much English, he had arrived in New Haven on a ship and was anxious to learn to read and write. Soon he was taken to Andover where Leonard Woods Sr. and others were starting their new seminary. For four years Opukaha'ia remained in and around Andover. In that first year, 1811, Opukaha'ia converted to Christianity. As news of him spread, he became a powerful witness to evangelicals in New England that Pacific peoples were anxious for what New England Christians could share.[45] Also during that time, more Hawaiians began to show up in New England. In 1816 there were fifty to sixty Hawaiians, five of whom were much in the public eye for their desire to be educated and their willingness to become Christians. In 1818, philanthropists founded a special "heathen school" in Cornwall, Connecticut. Eventually many ethnicities came to the school, but, as John Demos notes, "Certainly it was built on the hopes of Obookiah (and others) for a mission to the Sandwich Islands."[46] In 1818, Opukaha'ia died, but his hope of sending Protestant missionaries back to his homeland was fulfilled the following year when two students of Leonard Woods Sr. left Boston to devote their lives to Hawaiians: Asa Thurston, and the second, Hiram Bingham, the namesake of the "Mr. Bingham" that Dana knew in San Diego.

This brings us back to the writing of *Two Years Before the Mast* in 1838. During the voyage Dana had kept bare facts about his trip in a short notebook. In leisure hours on the boat and on Point Loma he wrote a fuller

---

44. There were, beginning probably 1789, Hawaiians serving as crew on board American ships. In 1801, an Hawaiian boy who had come in on a ship, had portrayed a Hawaiian in Boston in a play about Captain Cook. See Samuel E. Morison, "Boston Traders in Hawaiian Islands, 1789–1823."

45. See Bendroth, *A School of the Church*, 59–60; Hutchinson, *Errand into the World*, 67, *Memoirs of Henry Obookiah*, ed. Edwin W. Dwight, later edited by Edith Wolfe (Honolulu: Women's Board of Missions for the Pacific Islands, 2012); and Christopher L. Cook, *The Providential Life & Heritage of Henry Obookiah: Why Did Missionaries Come to Hawai'i from New England and Tahiti?* (Waimea, Kaua'I, Hawai'i: Pa'a Studios: 2015).

46. John Demos, *The Heathen School: A Story of Hope and Betrayal in the Age of the Early Republic* (New York: Vintage, 2014) 32.

account of some events, probably planning to write a book. When he returned to Boston in September of 1836 this fuller account was lost. Having re-ignited his commitment to an evangelical form of Christianity by the end of 1836, Dana spent 1837 finishing his Harvard undergraduate degree. During the first year of law school in 1838, Dana wrote *Two Years Before the Mast* drawing from his perfunctory notebook and his letters home.

Although we should be careful to read with an eye to Dana's necessity to reimagine the California coast, there is no reason to doubt the book's account of Dana finding happiness and purpose for himself while living with the colony of Hawaiians at *La Playa* on Point Loma. Four years after returning to Boston he published, to his astonishment, a run-away best seller. For the next half century, the book sold amazingly well, not only as a boy-coming-of-age adventure story, but also as a lesson in opportunity for Americans, not just opportunity for wealth in the West, but also opportunity to do good in the Pacific. For all the varied stories of people and places in the book, Americans with an evangelical bent could read a clear, calm, and loving group portrait of Hawaiians. The book is a classic and therefore can be read many times from many perspectives. However, a straight-up knowledge of Dana's life circumstances illuminates an appealing evangelical consciousness within the book. Dana went to California prepared to love Hawaiians and returned prepared to write a book, in part, about Hawaiians.[47] Yes, Dana did say in his book that white people had been a "curse" in the Pacific; however, Dana offered his own experience with Hawaiians in support of what evangelical Protestants wanted to hear: "The history of no people on the globe, can show anything like so rapid an advance" as the Hawaiians. The story of Dana's friendship with Mr. Bingham, Tom Davis, Pelican, and Hope on a small Mexican beach on Point Loma was not a heroic missionary tale; however, it embeds a redemptive and positive story at the center of an often despairing narrative about what awaits a sailor on the far side of the world.[48]

---

47. The issue of what Dana intended with his narrative has been much discussed. I add this "evangelical" intention to the mix of issues. See Robert F. Lucid, "*Two Years before the Mast* as Propaganda," *American Quarterly* 12 (1960) 392–403. See also the introductions to newer editions of the book by Gary Kinder (Modern Library, 2001), Thomas Philbrick (Penguin Classics, 1981), and John Seelye, with "Afterward" by Wright Morris (Signet Classic, 1964).

48. Dana Jr., *Two Years*, 19:160. What has become the classic introduction to the book upon which all modern introductions draw, including Starr's, is James D. Hart's "The Education of Richard Henry Dana Jr.," *New England Quarterly* 9 (1936) 3–25. This and the best biographies of Dana give due emphasis to Dana's evangelical fervor

By looking at the circumstances of Dana's introduction to the network of evangelical hopes and responsibility to the Hawaiians in 1832, we can see that when Dana met Hawaiians in 1835 outside the heavy surf in Santa Barbara, he was well-prepared to expect a relationship with them similar to the good relationship Prof. Woods had with Opukaha'ia. He possibly had read, or had read to him during his period of weak eyesight, Opukaha'ia's very popular short autobiography published in Boston. In that autobiography Opukaha'ia and his editor wrote of things Dana also wrote about: Hawaiians as fast learners, good mimics, full of playfulness and ingenuity, translation from English to Hawaiian, and Hawaiians studying geography/maps.[49]

If we come with an evangelical and Hawaiian perspective to the writing of *Two Years Before the Mast* in 1838, there are also some literary models for Dana that become evident that hitherto have not been noticed by scholars who have studied this classic of maritime literature. Given that the book was a major influence on Herman Melville, interest in Dana's models have long been of much interest.[50] The most available model to Dana was *Journal of Voyages and Travels by the Rev. Daniel Tyerman and George Bennet, Esq., Deputed from the London Missionary Society . . . Between the Years of 1821 and 1829* which was first published in London and republished in Boston and New York in 1832. This missionary-adventure-cultural anthropology book was widely popular even though it was three volumes long. The

---

throughout his life but do not emphasize, as I do, the role of Hawaiians as an indicator of that evangelical fervor before the book and in the book. These best biographies are Charles Francis Adams, *Richard Henry Dana: A Biography*, 2 vols. (Boston: Houghton, Mifflin, 1890); Samuel Shapiro, *Richard Henry Dana, Jr. 1815–1882* (East Lansing: Michigan State University Press, 1961); Jeffrey L. Amestoy, *Slavish Shore: The Odyssey of Richard Henry Dana Jr.* (Cambridge: Harvard University Press, 2015). This newest biography of Dana is an excellent study of Dana's life and importance as a lawyer, culminating in analysis of the national importance of Dana's sense of justice and mercy when serving as prosecutor of Jefferson Davis after the Civil War.

49. For comparisons: quick learners, see Dana Jr., *Two Years Before the Mast*, 19:161, and *Memoirs of Henry Obookiah*, 14; mimics, see Dana Jr., *Two Years Before the Mast*, 19:163, and *Memoirs*, 11, 13; playful and ingenuity, see Dana Jr., *Two Years Before the Mast*, throughout chapters 19 and 20, and *Memoirs*, 19; language translation, see Dana, *Two Years Before the Mast*, 19:158, and *Memoirs*, 31; geography/map: see Dana, *Two Years*, 19:162, and *Memoirs*, 26, 57.

50. See Robert F. Lucid, "The Influence of *Two Years Before the Mast* on Herman Melville," in *American Literature* 31 (1959) 243–56, and James D. Hart, "Melville and Dana," *American Literature* 9 (1937). I should here acknowledge my great debt in this essay to James D. Hart (1911–1990) and Robert F. Lucid (1930–2006).

American editor, who designates himself as R. A., wrote in the first lines of the preface that that Atlantic merchants had been a curse in the Pacific: "Until ministers of the gospel visited the Pacific, the progress of society, in all the islands which have since been evangelized, was downward, and with a rapidity which commerce did but accelerate." British and American commerce was a problem. But this was not a book that merely bemoans commerce and praises missionaries. No, the American editor writes that he is confident that readers will enjoy the wide ranging material in the book and recommends it especially to young people. In it there is much about "topographical delineations and descriptions of natural scenery." What is most important is that "MAN is the grand subject of their [the missionaries'] inquiries . . . and not a little of what is related concerning him is in the attractive form of anecdote."[51] The three volumes are an easy-to-read narrative full of anecdotes about sailing, sabbaths at sea, and whales, about pleasant days, storms, and about landfall on exotic islands including Hawaii, about cultures and government on those islands. There is, as with Dana's *Two Years Before the Mast*, a death at sea, a funeral for a child, fishing for sharks, amazement at the swimming feats of an Hawaiian, and a favorite Hawaiian friend who is named after a ship. Although the Tyerman and Bennet journal has none of the maritime technology celebrated by Dana, nor has it the intensity of Dana's pursuit of justice for sailors, the pace, descriptive character, and good intentions of their missionary-adventure story is similar to Dana's *Two Years Before the Mast*.[52]

In conclusion, I confess to being highly attracted to the Catholic and Aristotelian perspective evident often in Kevin Starr's multi-volume study of California culture.[53] Starr's religious perspective enhances his many vol-

---

51. "Preface to the American Edition," in *Journal of the Voyages and Travels by the Rev. Daniel Tyerman and George Bennet, Esq., Deputed from the London Missionary Society . . . between the Years 1821 and 1829*, compiled by James Montgomery, 3 vols. (Boston, 1832) v–viii.

52. Compare Dana Jr.'s *Two Years Before the Mast* also with Washington Irving's *Astoria: Anecdotes of an Enterprise beyond The Rocky Mountains* published in 1836. Irving's is an account of Americans in 1811 developing trade relations with Hawaii with "King Tamaahamaah." See also Ed Towse, "Some Hawaiians Abroad," *Papers of the Hawaiian Historical Society* 11 (1904) 3–22.

53. Kevin Starr received his BA from the University of San Francisco (1962) and is presently on the Board of Trustees of the Institute for Advanced Catholic Studies at the University of Southern California. The website of the Dominican School of Philosophy and Theology in Berkeley, California describes Starr: "Throughout his distinguished career he has never hesitated publicly to profess his Catholic faith. In his work in

umes and gives him clearer perspective about what California has meant to people in American history. Starr is right to see prophetic roots of California's Protestant culture in *Two Years Before the Mast* and the mentality of its author; however, Starr did not see the specific, evangelical culture, that Dana appealed to when writing about Hawaiians. If we put Dana's *Two Years Before the Mast* in the context of Charles Foster's *An Errand of Mercy: The Evangelical United Front 1790–1837*, the depiction of the Hawaiians at *La Playa* on Point Loma in 1835–36 becomes more central to understanding what Dana wanted to say about the future of California and what the new Californians after the 1850s wanted to hear. If we read the book from an evangelical perspective, we can see that *La Playa* is portrayed as a beachhead, the first landing in California, of a dynamic evangelical do-good and save-the-world culture. Evangelical progressivism would later thrive on the California coast and become leading influences in American culture and politics. Prophetically, a young Bostonian depicted himself during the Mexican period of California history as an idealistic and conflicted young man who found evangelical purpose among a small colony of Hawaiians. Hundreds, eventually thousands of readers would come to California with similar evangelical hopes of finding similar purpose and fellowship.

---

communications and in his civic responsibilities he has manifested the truth that the 'mixed life,' a life that seeks to contemplate the truth, and yet to teach and encourage others, is the highest calling of the Christian. Kevin encourages and promotes the work of the laity in the Church; he is currently working on the publication of his book *Lift Up Your Hearts: The American Catholic Experience*." (https://www.dspt.edu/kevin-starr, accessed February 2016).

Beating the Unbeatable Foe

Anti-Communism and Fear of Subversion in Southern California in the 1960s

WILLIAM KATERBERG

ANTI-COMMUNISM SEEMS QUAINT TO most Americans today. Some have heard of the John Birch Society (JBS), but most know little about it. The Christian Anti-Communist Crusade (CACC) and Fred Schwarz are mostly forgotten, getting brief mention in studies of conservative religious and political movements in the 1950s and 1960s.[1] Fragments of scholarship and the rare dissertation connect them to "far right" movements in the postwar era and to the interconnected world of conservative politics in Southern California. That world included local Republican politicians and activists, religious conservatives, and Hollywood celebrities such as Fred Murphy and Ronald Reagan, both prominent future politicians in California and beyond.[2]

---

1. For example, Lisa McGirr, *Suburban Warriors: The Origins of the New American Right* (Princeton: Princeton University Press, 2001); and Kurt Schuparra, *Triumph of the Right: The Rise of the California Conservative Movement, 1945–1966* (Armonk, NY: Sharpe, 1998).

2. Samuel Lawrence Brenner, *Shouting at the Rain: The Voices and Ideas of Right-Wing Anti-Communist Americanists in the Era of Modern American Conservatism, 1950–1974*, PhD diss., Brown University, 2009; Clyde Wilcox, "Popular Backing for the Old Christian Right," *Journal of Social History* 21, no. 1 (1987) 117–32; and Raymond E. Wolfinger et al., "America's Radical Right," in *Ideology and Discontent*, ed. David E. Apter (New York: Free, 1964) 262–93. Just out is Nicole Hemmer, *Messengers of the Right: Conservative Media and the Transformation of American Politics* (Philadelphia: University of Pennsylvania Press, 2016).

Anti-Communists like Schwarz merit serious attention, however, as historical phenomena and as means to think about fear of subversion in American political culture more generally. Polemicists and journalists from the 1960s certainly took them seriously, depicting them as threats to American freedom and democracy.[3] Schools of anti-communism organized by the CACC in Los Angeles in the late summer and early fall of 1961, and the response to them, reveal the character of far right fears, their institutional character, networks, and use of media, the extent of their influence, and fears about them.

The Southern California School of Anti-Communism and a TV special at the Hollywood Bowl special represented a high point in the growth and influence of the CACC and brought Fred Schwarz notoriety. Anti-communist organizations such as the CACC and JBS flourished into the mid-1960s, as millions of Americans feared the threat of international Communism and internal subversion within the United States. Their success inspired concern among moderate and progressive Americans that anti-communist organizations were an "extremist," "far right," and perhaps fascist threat to the American way of life.

This essay explores the work of Schwarz and the CACC, in regional and national contexts. The CACC's history offers a window into recurring right-wing movements in the twentieth and early twenty-first century, from its own time to the Moral Majority, the Christian Coalition and the Tea Party, and their evolution from anti-Communism to the "culture wars." Such movements and their opponents typically have viewed each other as threats to the American way of life, envisioning themselves as the nation's mainstream and the other as extremist and subversive.

Background

Schwarz was born in Brisbane, Australia in 1913, the son of Jewish convert to Christianity who migrated from Vienna to England and then to Australia. Young Fred dedicated himself to Christ in the 1930s, earned a BA, and taught math and science at an "industrial school." In 1940s, he went to medical school and became a doctor, specializing in psychiatry. During

---

3. For example, Richard Dudman, *Men of the Far Right* (New York: Pyramid, 1962); Milton A. Waldor, *Peddlers of Fear* (Garden City, NY: Doubleday, 1964); Arnold Forster and Benjamin Epstein, *Danger on the Right* (New York: Random House, 1964); and Philip Horton, "Revivalism on the Far Right," *The Reporter* 25 (20 July 1961) 25–29.

these years, he helped found "the Christian Revelers," whose Saturday night rallies in Brisbane featured "hearty singing and clapping" and bold preaching, and he debated communists on university campuses.[4]

Schwarz drew the attention of two North American fundamentalists, Carl McIntyre and T. T. Shields. Schwarz himself notes that both men were "controversial" and would have been labeled extremists if the term had been common in 1950.[5] They invited him to speak about the dangers of Communism to American churches. On his tour, he became acquainted with William Pietsch, a radio preacher from Iowa. In 1953 the two men formed the CACC, urged on by Billy Graham. The CACC's mission was "[to] combat communism by means of lectures in schools, colleges, civic clubs, servicemen's organization and other similar organizations and through radio and television broadcasts and by providing courses for missionaries and others to be used in Bible schools and seminaries and the holding of religious and evangelistic services in churches, and through the publication of books, pamphlets and other literature and by all other appropriate means."[6] The CACC was active in the US and abroad, in India and British Guiana, and later Vietnam and Thailand, doing evangelistic missions and teaching about the evils of communism.

In 1956 Pietsch and Schwarz moved the organization to Long Beach. Southern California was a media center with a long history of successful religious entrepreneurs, from Aimee Semple McPherson to Robert Shuler. It had a large local population of well-organized, religious and political conservatives who would provide an audience and the small donations and membership fees that were the bread and butter of the CACC. And it had well-heeled donors who could fund and promote the media endeavors of an ambitious and entrepreneurial Schwartz.[7]

The CACC must be placed in the longer contexts of fundamentalism and anti-communism in the US. A fundamentalist is "an evangelical who is angry about something," Jerry Falwell once quipped. A strong emphasis on apologetics and debate also characterizes fundamentalism. The anti-Communist "ministry" of Fred Schwarz and the CACC likewise emphasized that

---

4. See Schwarz, *Beating the Unbeatable Foe: One Man's Victory over Communism, Leviathan, and the Last Enemy* (Washington, DC: Regnery, 1996) 15–40.

5. Schwarz, *Beating the Unbeatable Foe*, 40, 42.

6. Quoted in Foster and Epstein, *Danger on the Right*.

7. See Darren Dochuk, *From Bible Belt to Sunbelt: Plain Folk Religion, Grassroots Politics, and the Rise of Evangelical Conservatism* (New York: Norton, 2010).

ideas determine human action. They militantly defended truth, criticized heresy and falsehood, and diagnosed those who disagreed as ill, insane, or evil. With evangelicalism, more generally, fundamentalism has inspired entrepreneurial leaders and organizations.[8] The CACC also built on "Old Right" anti-Communist movements that go back to the Red Scare after World War I and in response to the success of labor unions, Communist and other leftwing organizing, and FDR's New Deal in the 1930s.[9] Anti-Communist efforts were promoted much more widely from the 1920s to the 1950s, of course, by J. Edgar Hoover and the FBI, Congressional bodies such as the House Un-American Activities Committee (established in 1938), and by various Protestant, Roman Catholic, African American, and Jewish groups, and even anti-Communist socialists. Whatever labels others applied to them—"extremist," "far right," or "fascist"—militants like Schwarz viewed themselves simply as defending "Americanism."[10]

In the 1950s and 1960s, the CACC was only one of a number of militant Christian and secular anti-Communist organizations. "Far right" anti-Communism suffered from apocalypse-mongering, conspiracy-minded activists, whose fantastic, often anti-Semitic scenarios discredited more careful anti-Communists, who pointed more specifically to Communist activity internationally and in the US itself. Robert W. Welch, Jr., for example, who founded the John Birch Society (JBS) in 1958, notoriously claimed that President Eisenhower was "a conscious, dedicated agent of the communist conspiracy." Where "mainstream" conservatives saw blundering, blindness, and stupidity among government officials and other Americans who denied the dangers of Communism to the American way of life, "extremists" on the "far right" saw conspiracies at work, notably in the State Department and military and among elected officials. Schwarz and the CACC straddled

---

8. Falwell is quoted in George Marsden, *Fundamentalism and American Culture*, 2nd ed. (New York: Oxford University Press, 2006) 235. "Mainline" denominations suffered a religious "depression" in the 1930s, declining; fundamentalist institutions grew during these years. See Joel A. Carpenter, *Revive Us Again: The Reawakening of American Fundamentalism* (New York: Oxford University Press, 1997).

9. Wilcox, "Popular Backing," 117.

10. See Richard Gid Powers, *Not without Honor: The History of American Anti-Communism* (New York: Free, 1995); and Leo P. Ribuffo, *The Old Christian Right: The Protestant Far Right from the Great Depression to the Cold War* (Philadelphia: Temple University Press, 1983). On anti-Communism uniting conservatives, see Gerald Nash, *The Conservative Intellectual Movement in America since 1945* (New York: Basic, 1976).

this line and worked to find support in the varied and often conflicting communities and institutions of the anti-Communist world.[11]

Fred Schwarz and the CACC

The core message of the CACC did not change from the 1950s to the mid-1960s. Schwarz used the language of the pathologist, saying that the disease of Communism had to be diagnosed correctly to be defeated. The communist formula for global conquest was simple: "External encirclement, plus internal demoralization, leads to progressive surrender." Communist military and political expansion globally was a real danger, Schwarz agreed, pointing to Eastern Europe, China, North Korea, Indo-China, Cuba, and dangers in newly independent colonies around the globe. But the deeper danger was "internal demoralization," a lack of moral resolve and intellectual clarity at home.[12]

The key to understanding the cunning of Communism was not its atheism or materialism but its notion of a dialectic in history—or as Schwarz put it in one of his stock lectures, "Communist Philosophy: The Difficult, Devious, and Dangerous Dialectic."[13] "According to the dialectic," he explained, "the driving force in any situation is the conflict of two opposing forces. Thesis and antithesis. Nothing exists in isolation."[14] Communists used deceptive tactical shifts that seemed to depart from Communism, but really were temporary expediencies. Communism always remained the goal. In the 1920s, Lenin allowed peasants to farm individually. Stalin promoted "common fronts" against fascism in the 30s and 40s. Khrushchev and Brezhnev promoted nuclear arms reduction and détente in the 60s and 70s. Schwarz often used the analogy of a hammer, where the backswing of the tool readied it for next strike of the nail, not a reversal of intention or

---

11. Redekop, *The American Far Right*, is useful on this point. Welch is quoted in Powers, *Not without Honor*, 314.

12. CACC Newsletter, November 1954, http://www.schwarzreport.org/uploads/schwarz-report-pdf/the-schwarz-report-november-19541.pdf (accessed 18 June 2010). Some newsletters can be found online; many more are in a microfilm collection produced by Proquest, *The Right Wing Collection of the University of Iowa Libraries 1918–1977*. See http://www.proquest.com/en-US/catalogs/collections/detail/Right-Wing-Collection-of-University-of-Iowa-Libraries-362.shtml.

13. *Beating the Unbeatable Foe*, 168.

14. *You Can Trust the Communists* (Englewood Cliffs, NJ: Prentice-Hall, 1960) 157.

long term course.[15] In the 1990s, Schwarz insisted that global Communist conquest remained official goal of China, even as it seemed to embrace capitalism. Communists could not be judged on the basis of what they said or did in any given moment. They hid their true intentions.

Part of the appeal of Communism, Schwarz argued, was the psychology of the dialectic, the satisfaction enjoyed by true-believing Communists that they alone are truly in the know, "people of a special mold" to whom the course of history had been revealed. Communists believed that "*they discern the origins of the forces and the laws by which those forces operate. This enables them to influence the consequences [of events] and to predict the future accurately.*"[16]

The same psychological dynamic was true of anti-Communism. Unlike liberal politicians and foolish intellectuals, who were dupes of Communism, militant anti-Communists truly were in the know. They understood the malevolent nature of their foe and saw clearly the course of history, one that threatened to sweep up an America that only seemed secure and strong.[17]

Communism was not just a political danger, but a cosmic evil. Scwharz's writings linked the day-to-day events of the Cold War to cosmic history. Schwarz trusted that God and those who followed God's ways ultimately would defeat Communism and the Satanic forces behind it. His pessimism about Communism should be read as a "jeremiad," a warning against sliding into indolence and a call to arms to convince people to follow God and take up the battle against the foe, a foe that during the Cold War was Communism, but ultimately was an eternal enemy.[18]

Schwarz and his organization took up the moral and intellectual battle against the Communist foe in public lectures to high schools, colleges, civic

---

15. CACC Newsletter, June 1960 http://www.schwarzreport.org/uploads/schwarz-report-pdf/schwarz-report-1960-06.pdf (accessed 15 July 2010).

16. *Beating the Unbeatable Foe*, 67, 68.

17. See the CACC Newsletter, September 1958, in which he reported on a speech he gave in Washington, DC, entitled: "Will the Kremlin Conquer America by the Year 1973?," http://www.schwarzreport.org/uploads/schwarz-report-pdf/schwarz-report-1958-09.pdf (accessed 15 July 2010); and see the CACC Newsletter for May 1959, http://www.schwarzreport.org/uploads/schwarz-report-pdf/schwarz-report-1959-05.pdf (accessed 15 July 2010).

18. On this cosmic sensibility, see Paul Boyer, *When Time Shall Be No More: Prophecy Belief in Modern American Culture* (Cambridge, MA: Harvard University Press, 1994). On the jeremiad, see Sacvan Bercovitch, *The American Jeremiad* (Madison: University of Wisconsin Press, 1978).

organizations, business groups, military audiences, and more. He testified before HAUC in February 1953, and the CACC published his testimony in ads in the *New York Times, Washington Post, Los Angeles Times*, and many smaller papers. Wealthy supporters paid for the ads and for offprints of Schwarz's testimony for high schools. The CACC eagerly used media opportunities like this, where testimony by Schwarz was a public document and so could be introduced into school curricula. The CACC also distributed material overseas, notably in India, where it ran a variety of anti-Communist and evangelistic missions.

In the spring of 1958 the CACC started a new venture, schools of anti-communism, the first one held in St. Louis. Schools began when local anti-Communists set up a committee to sponsor a school and invite the CACC. The local committee would take care of the logistics. The CACC would provide the program and faculty, who were free to express their own opinions. Donations raised by the local committee to pay for the school would go to the CACC because it had tax exempt status. The CACC would keep the surplus, and the local committee would disband after the school was completed. The "net" take for the Southern California school in 1961, for example, was about $200,000.[19]

Schwarz and the CACC generally avoided two of the day's major political issues: civil rights for African Americans and independence for colonies abroad. Schwarz was not overtly racist so much as indifferent. He occasionally noted that racial inequities such as denial of the right to vote were wrong. Yet he believed that race relations in the US generally were good and that European colonies had been largely content places. Like most anti-Communists, he claimed that Communists used civil rights groups to infiltrate the US and weaken America against the true danger of Communism. He also worried that newly independent former colonies might easily be taken over by Communists. When pressed on these issues he professed ignorance, saying that he was a specialist in Communism, and complaining that it was unreasonable to ask him about these other issues, like it would be unreasonable to expect a surgeon to know much about oncology.[20]

The CACC's programs and Schwarz's writings place them at the border between and "far right" and "mainstream" conservatives. CACC extremism can be seen in its defense of indoctrination. CACC speakers scorned the notion that Communists should treated the same way as other

---

19. See *Beating the Unbeatable Foe*, 243.
20. For example, see ibid., 238–39.

Americans, their views be listened to and judged like any other point of view. Advocates of judging Communism objectively "adorn themselves with the garments of academic righteousness," he complained, "and attack those who would teach Communism as a completely evil system as advocates of indoctrination, not education." Such people failed to see Communism as a moral and intellectual disease and Communists sick and evil. The notion that Communism could be treated like any other set of ideas "is false and represents academic infantilism rather than maturity," Schwarz insisted. "Education without basic indoctrination is impossible."[21] There is right and wrong, truth and falsehood, sanity and insanity, and Communism should be tolerated intellectually no more than the claim that 2+2=5. And only those who were ideologically pure could be trusted to convey truth and be reasonable.[22]

Schwarz's stance was common among "extreme" anti-Communists, but it is noteworthy that he avoided accusing individuals of being part of active Communist conspiracies, unlike Joseph McCarthy in the 1950s and Welch, the JBS, and others on the "far right" in the 1960s. "Guest faculty" at CACC schools, who often also worked with the JBS, often did name alleged traitors and fellow travelers in the State Department and other places of high influence in government.[23] It is likely that many people who attended CACC school also participated in JBS groups locally. Nonetheless, Schwarz complained mightily that lumping the CACC with the JBS amounted to "guilt by association," something liberals hated when their critics lumped them in with Communists.[24]

The Southern California School of Anti-Communism

The first school of anti-Communism run by the CACC, in St. Louis in 1958, attracted about 130 participants. In next few years, The CACC conducted dozens more schools across country, especially in the South, Midwest, and West (including Long Beach, Los Angeles, San Francisco,

21. CACC Newsletter, November 1963, http://www.schwarzreport.org/uploads/schwarz-report-pdf/schwarz-report-1963-11.pdf (accessed 30 July 2010).

22. See Hemmer, *Messengers of the Right*, on this theme.

23. See the CACC newsletter for April 1962, http://www.schwarzreport.org/uploads/schwarz-report-pdf/schwarz-report-1962-04.pdf (accessed 29 July 2010).

24. Schwarz was still complaining decades later, in his autobiography; see *Beating the Unbeatable Foe*, 181–82.

Houston, Dallas, San Diego, Phoenix, Seattle, and Portland). By the early 1960s the schools were attracting thousands of participants, raising money for the CACC, signing up members, and starting local study groups. Amid some controversy, local Navy officers helped organize a school at the Glenview Naval Air Station in Chicago.[25] During the summer of 1961, in the weeks before the Southern California School in LA, the CACC held a successful school in nearby Orange County, attracting over 12,000 students to the "Youth Night."[26]

The Southern California School, held in the Memorial Sports Arena in LA from 28 August to 1 September 1961, received major support from wealth local business leaders and the LA Chamber of Commerce. Actor George Murphy was the MC for the school's evening events, which drew 5,000 people to the first evening and 10,000 to the last evening, according to the October CACC newsletter. The Youth Night attracted 18,000, leaving thousands more outside wanting in. The Richfield Oil Company sponsored TV broadcasts of the evening events, which drew an audience of 3,000,000 people nightly. Schwarz praised the TV and live audience years later, saying that the enthusiasm they showed for his message, approach, and jokes, and the focused attention they paid, "proved that those who accused Americans of having a short attention span were deluded." Over the course of the school, the "attendance at the Sports Arena increased and the television ratings were high."[27] It featured Republican politicians such as Senator Thomas Dodd of Connecticut and Representative Walter Judd of Minnesota. Ronald Reagan, Roy Rogers, and Pat Boone made appearances at the Youth Night event. "The immediate result" of the school (beyond net revenue of over $200,000) "has been the formation of literally thousands of study groups in the Southern California area," the newsletter noted. "Already the effects are being felt in the Bay Region by local people who attended the school and by the fact that one of the local television stations has expressed its desire to cover a local school when it is held." The coverage of the LA *Times* was circumspect. But in a column in the *Examiner*, Vincent Flaherty gushed: "The Anti-Communism School founded here very well may be a powerful nationwide antidote to shake the country

---

25. CACC Newsletter, October 1960, http://www.schwarzreport.org/uploads/schwarz-report-pdf/schwarz-report-1960-10.pdf (accessed 15 July 2010).

26. See the CACC newsletter for April/May 1961, http://www.schwarzreport.org/uploads/schwarz-report-pdf/schwarz-report-1961-05.pdf (accessed 15 July 2010).

27. *Beating the Unbeatable Foe*, 215.

out of its 11th hour complacency. It is almost certain to sweep into other large population areas, increasing the momentum it developed here."[28] Indeed, local CACC supporters in the San Francisco Bay Area had already begun to organize and raise money for a school there. It would be held in Oakland in early 1962.

The school also inspired strong criticism. *Life Magazine* described the CACC as "Far Right Revivalists" in an article published on the last day of the school. "A new kind of 'revival meeting' serving the nonreligious ends of an outfit called the 'Christian Anti-Communism Crusade' is being held," it said, "with full hullabaloo and political portent in Los Angeles this week." *Life* criticized Schwarz's "doomsday" preaching, accusing him of asking "every American" to start "distrusting his neighbor as a possible Communist or 'consymp' (Communist sympathizer)." It noted the he "tries to appear less extreme" than the JBS and "publically disavows Birchism," but claimed that the local steering committees that organized CACC schools of included Birchers. *Life* also implied that the schools were a get-rich-quick scheme for the CACC, noting that Schwarz planned to take the show on the road to parts East (Chicago, New York, and Washington).[29] The December CACC newsletter responded by quoting a "prominent psychologist" who dismissed the *Life* article as characterized by "brain washing," "smear tactics," and "malicious intent," as so many stories on organizations like the CACC do. "[The] writer," the unnamed psychologist wrote, may not be "a Communist or even a pro-Communist: he may simply have been brainwashed himself into feeling what he wrote was 'news' and served to decrease anti-Communist 'hysteria.'"[30]

The CACC apparently was not alone in responding angrily. *Life* received enough complaints, and perhaps cancelled subscriptions, that Schwarz later met with the owner of *Life* and *Time* magazines, Henry Luce.[31] In October, Luce forced the publisher of *Life* and vice president of *Time*, Inc., C.D. Jackson, to apologize publically to Schwarz and the CACC. On October 16, Jackson took the stage at the Hollywood Bowl as part of a three-hour televised event called "Hollywood's Answer to Communism."

28. See Brenner, "Shouting at the Rain," 215; and Schwarz, *Beating the Unbeatable Foe*, 220.

29. "Far Right Revivalists," *Life* (1 September 1961) 39.

30. CACC Newsletter for December 1961, http://www.schwarzreport.org/uploads/schwarz-report-pdf/schwarz-report-1961–12.pdf (accessed 11 September 2010).

31. Schwarz, *Beating the Unbeatable Foe*, 221ff.

The CACC had organized the TV special as a follow-up to the Southern California School. The article was filled with "oversimplified misinformation" and "misinterpretation," "Jackson said. "We were wrong, and I am profoundly sorry." In February 1962, *Time* printed a story called "Crusader Schwarz," which Schwarz thought was better. "I had only one criticism, which I made reluctantly," Schwarz wrote years later in his autobiography. "Apparently the talented journalists of *Time* magazine did not fully understand the limited role of the pathologist in the treatment of disease." Schwarz believed that the article wrongly faulted him for merely diagnosing the problem of Communism without giving his audiences a remedy. This was how he defined his work and that of the CACC: a program of education intended to diagnose the threat of communism. It was up to others to treat the disease.[32]

At the Hollywood Bowl extravaganza, a "color guard" of 350 Boy Scouts helped open the evening. Actor George Murphy, who would win a seat in the US Senate in 1964, once again served as master of ceremonies. The night included speeches by Schwarz himself, Cleon Skousen (a former FBI employee), Senator Dodd, and Representative Judd. Celebrities who made appearances included John Wayne, Pat Boone, Roy Rogers, Jimmy Stewart, Donna Reed, Ronald Reagan, and Ozzie and Harriet Nelson. "Boone in particular received a 'ringing ovation' when he told the audience that he would rather see his four girls 'shot and die as little girls who have faith in God than have them die some years later as godless, faithless, soulless Communists.'"[33] For his part, the repentant Jackson further said, "It's a great privilege to be here tonight to align *Life* magazine with Sen. Dodd, Rep. Judd, Dr. Schwarz, and the rest of these implacable fighters" against communism. The *Los Angeles Herald-Express* observed with thanks that these celebrities had shown the "guts" to fight against the "Communist infiltration" of Hollywood. Over thirty TV stations broadcast the show, which was sponsored by Richfield Oil and Schick Razors. The event drew over 15,000 people to the Hollywood Bowl, and some four million people in six Western states watched the show on TV. The CACC taped the event and rebroadcast it on TV stations in other parts of the country in the following months.[34]

---

32. For the quotations, see Schwarz, *Beating the Unbeatable Foe*, 228–29, 225.
33. Brenner, "Shouting at the Rain," 1.
34. Ibid., 3–4; Schwarz, *Beating the Unbeatable Foe*, 226ff.

A study of a CACC school held in Oakland, California in early 1962 offers a window into how audiences view its message. The researchers used interviews and mail-in questionnaires. The cost of the school was $20 for the week, but clergy, teachers, students, police, fire fighters, and military personnel received a half-price discount. Free passes, or "scholarships," meant that about 30 percent of the study's "respondents did not pay for their tickets." Some attendees directed "suspicion, hostility, and abuse" at the interviewers.[35] Other used the interview as an opportunity to convert the researchers, students in particular. The study, published in 1964, rejected the social-psychological explanations common at the time about the "far right," which pointed to "status anxiety," an "authoritarian personality," and "alienation" to explain their influence. Fundamentalist beliefs corresponded better than these factors, but not enough to draw strong conclusions.[36] "The most economical answer" to the question of who supported the CACC, the study stated, is that it "draws its support from Republicans, chiefly those of higher socioeconomic status." These supporters were best characterized by disgruntlement with Republican leaders who supported the welfare state. "Communism" seems to have been a "shorthand symbol for unacceptable political trends." The fact that the Republicans were out of power in 1962 may have invigorated the CACC and organizations like it, as "fears about the influence of anti-Communism" in the late 1950s "were restrained . . . by the improbability that Eisenhower was soft on communism." With Kennedy's Democrats in power in 1962, "anticommunism" was "a way to express resentment with maximum emotional impact and a minimum of divisiveness within the Republican Party."[37]

A study from the 1980s also rejected social-psychological explanations for the growth of the CACC, but framed the CACC in a longer historical context.[38] The "Christian Right" of the 1960s "rose from the same roots" as that "of the 1920s," it concluded. "Both movements were spawned during the enthusiasm of fundamentalist religious activity which had begun with a more purely religious focus and then spread to political concerns

---

35. Wolfinger et al, "America's Radical Right," 265–66.

36. Three-quarters of the CACC school attendees were Protestant. The regular churchgoers in the sample tended to be more "liberal" on domestic issues than non-churchgoers—e.g., on issues such as segregation, public medical care for the "aged," and federal funding of education. Among the non-churchgoers, low income people were as conservative on these issues as moderate to higher income people. See ibid., 282.

37. Ibid., "America's Radical Right," 288.

38. Wilcox, "Popular Backing for the Old Christian Right," 123–27.

... Both embraced anti-communism, which found fertile soil in the minds of fundamentalists predisposed by doctrine to associate the Soviet Union with the forces of the anti-Christ."[39] Both also had complex attitudes toward modernization, embracing capitalism and modern technology, but rejecting as immoral, unchristian, "worldly," and a threat to Christian freedom many of the ideas and socio-cultural trends associated with contemporary life in the 1960s, notably changes in gender, sexuality, and family life. The same was true of the Moral Majority, the Christian Right of the 1980s.

The Southern California school and Hollywood Bowl extravaganza marked a high point for the CACC. This success quickly inspired fear among critics that organizations like the CACC were extremist and a threat to American institutions and values. Spurred on by the notoriety it received in the press, the CACC continued to grow in the next few years. This criticism had immediate consequences, however, for the CACC, even if anti-Communist organizing did not go into marked decline after the failed presidential campaign of Barry Goldwater in 1964.

Anti-Anti-Communism and the Decline of the CACC

Criticism of anti-Communism was as old as anti-Communism itself, but attacks on the CACC came thick and fast in 1961 and 1962. Moderates and progressives feared that "far right" anti-Communists represented a threat to the American way of life. It is too simple to say that the conflict over anti-Communism was partisan—as Democratic politicians sometimes spoke on CACC programs—but there is something to such a generalization. The CACC officially was non-partisan, and Schwarz avoided partisanship in public events. Yet support for and opposition to organizations like the CACC were highly partisan. The most militant, obsessive anti-Communists tended to be Republicans, and the most strident anti-anti-Communists tended to be Democrats. In responding to criticism, Schwarz himself cited the "party loyalties" of "liberals" as a factor, albeit without acknowledging the partisan nature of his own supporters and movement.[40]

Evidence for the partisan nature of the attacks is clear, even if there was no coordinated effort against anti-Communists. In August 1961, the Democratic chairman of the Senate Foreign Relations Committee William

39. Ibid., 129.
40. *Beating the Unbeatable Foe*, 252.

Fulbright published in the *Congressional Record* a memo on the propaganda activities of military personnel, addressing it to the Department of Defense. He focused on the anti-Communism efforts of high-ranking officers who sometimes used materials adapted from "far right" organizations and on programs meant for soldiers run by "right-wing speakers."[41] In November 1961 in Los Angeles, President Kennedy criticized "far right" groups. According to Schwarz, he "seemed to endorse the delusions of Senator Fullbright," giving "momentum" to the "campaign of misinformation and slander against the Crusade." Walter Reuther, president of the United Auto Workers and an ally of the Kennedy administration, issued a memo on dangers of right-wing extremism, pointing to the CACC. The Democratic attorney general of California, Staley Mosk, mocked the CACC's claims to be a "school" in early 1962. It was licensed by no official body, he observed, its "faculty" not accredited or credentialed by anyone. Mosk depicted the CACC as a money-making venture, noting the large sums involved in the Southern California school and the cost of the books, pamphlets, and audio tapes it sold. "Patriotism for Profit," he alleged. Mosk also depicted CACC speakers as "shrill-voiced apostles of despair" who ignored all of the good being done the US government and successes in containing Communism. Schwarz had ready responses to such criticism, including clean bills of financial health from the IRS, but noted bitterly the effect of attacks by persons of "stature."[42]

The press and advocacy organizations such as the Anti-Defamation League also often lumped in the CACC with the JBS and other extremist groups. CBS filmed a CACC school in Florida in late 1961 and aired a TV news program on the organization in early 1962. The story, "Thunder on the Right," cherry-picked material "to confirm the pre-reached conclusion that the Crusade was a right-wing extremist organization," Schwarz complained. Similar stories in newspapers and magazines such as *Newsweek*, *Look*, and *The Reporter* accused the CACC of naming names and urging Americans to hunt for communists in their communities and institutions. Mainline clergy also got in on the act, in California and nationally. Some critics charged the CACC and Schwarz with anti-Semitism, noting that the organization eschewed membership by Jews and Roman Catholics.[43] Schwarz sued his critics on occasion, but as a public figure he

---

41. Ibid., 250–69.
42. Ibid., 279.
43. Schwarz expressed his fundamentalist religious beliefs carefully, downplaying

always lost. The best he got was the occasional apology from critics, when they got facts wrong.

The press was not universally hostile, of course. The LA *Examiner* and NY *Post*, and other conservative newspapers and magazines, continued to support the CACC and anti-Communism. A useful indication of where the CACC and Schwarz stood in the eyes of fellow conservatives and anti-Communists can be in seen in the defense of Schwarz by William Buckley and the *National Review*. The *National Review* distanced itself from and later condemned and ostracized the JBS from the conservative movement. In 1962, in "The Impending Smear of Fred Schwarz," Buckley argued that "the very special resentment against Schwarz has to do with his obstinate refusal to make a fool of himself." Schwarz did not engage in attacks on individuals or in conspiracy-mongering. "If *only* he would write a book calling Eisenhower a Communist, or announce that the White House staff is riddled with spies, or suggest that the Union Theological Seminary is a Communist front, or that the ultimate loyalty of Catholics is suspect, or that the Jews are a treasonable breed of men—with what a relief the anti-anti-Communists would greet the news."[44]

Despite such support, and despite thin evidence for many of the criticisms of the CACC, the onslaught had a practical impact on its programs. The CACC did not lose members, and it continued to raise money effectively until 1965 at least. But it lost access to State Department programs and invitations to speak on military bases disappeared, as did government funding of the translation and publication of CACC books and pamphlets for overseas distribution. The CACC also found it more difficult to rent time on TV stations to broadcast its programs. Schwarz thought that TV stations feared retribution by the FCC, given the Kennedy administrations hostility. More likely, the negative press about "extremism" made TV stations wary for prosaic market reasons. In any case, opposition by political opponents and criticism in the press changed the marketplace for the

---

them in books, pamphlets, and CACC schools in order to reach broad audiences and work with government organizations. CACC schools included Mormon, Roman Catholic, and Jewish speakers. The CACC was overtly pietistic, however, in its newsletters. When asked by Roman Catholics in the 1950s about cooperating with them, Schwarz suggested they establish their own organization, which they did—the Cardinal Mindszenty Foundation. Schwarz said that he favored religious freedom and diversity, not uniformity. See *Beating the Unbeatable Foe*, 320–22 and 164ff; and Donald T. Critchlow, *Phyllis Schlafly and Grassroots Conservatism* (Princeton: Princeton University Press, 2007).

44. Buckley, "The Impending Smear of Fred Schwarz," *National Review* (5 June 1962) 398; *Beating the Unbeatable Foe*, 326–30.

CACC. The Goldwater campaign in 1964 provided a temporary boost for militant anti-Communists, but his crushing defeat by Lyndon Johnson in the election and the emergence of new issues marginalized militant anti-Communist organizations like the CACC.

The CACC and the Later Sixties

The CACC struggled to address new challenges in the later 1960s. "The world has changed dramatically during the past decade," Schwarz observed in 1972. International Communism had fragmented with the Chinese-Soviet split. At home—notably in San Francisco, Oakland, and Berkeley in northern California—the Black Panthers, student radicals, the sexual revolution, women's rights, and counterculture spread chaos.[45] These movements seemed "bizarre and strange, with new life-styles accompanying new revolutionary movements."[46]

Schwarz diagnosed the new movements in *The Three Faces of Revolution*. Who could have imagined, he asked, "Kidnappings, riots in the ghettos, riots on campus, and mutiny in the armed forces"? Or that Americans born into privilege would form terrorist cells and "engage in an orgy of bombing and arson"? Some of the problems that revolutionaries pointed to were real, Schwarz admitted, but instead of bringing "reformation" to essentially good American institutions, or applying the wisdom of the gospel, revolutionaries brought destruction and promoted moral decline in service of communist revolution.[47] Schwarz continued to focus on ideas, stating "that the revolutionary words of yesterday have been followed by the revolutionary deeds of today."[48]

The new threats came in four forms, Schwarz explained: the "alienated," "reformers," "partisans," and "destroyers." The alienated were the "uprooted" youth of America, who had lost their "faith in reason" and become separated from families, homes, religion, and love of country.[49] Reformers

---

45. *Beating the Unbeatable Foe*, 371–72. On the counterculture and sexuality, see the CACC newsletter for April 17, 1967 http://www.schwarzreport.org/uploads/schwarz-report-pdf/schwarz-report-1967-04-17.pdf (accessed 3 August 2010).

46. Schwarz, *The Three Faces of Revolution* (Washington, DC: Capitol Hill, 1972) vii. The "three faces" were Communism, Anarchism, and Sensualism.

47. Ibid., viii.

48. Ibid., 1.

49. Ibid., 9.

worked for Hubert Humphrey or got "clean for Gene" in the Democratic presidential campaigns of 1968 and 1972. Partisans focused on specific grievances, "one special objective above all others"—women's liberationists, labor groups, peace activists, "The Homosexuals," and national minorities (who might unite in a "Third World Liberation Front").[50] These were the flammable materials of a communist "bomb" that threatened America. A small minority of revolutionaries, a mere 30,000 in the U.S. (Schwarz cited *Fortune* magazine), would set off the bomb in the coming revolution.[51] They were "destroyers." They had picked up the "torch" carried by their Communist forebears. Schwarz seems to have been confused by the anarchist energies of the late 1960s. The old enemy, Communism, was harder to perceive and popping up in unexpected places, with radicals and dupe supporters coming from every conceivable and inconceivable area of society.

The CACC adapted its methods and focus to meet the new threat faces of revolution. In 1966, it began to scale back its schools of anti-communism, which emphasized educating adults, and instead began to run "Anti-Subversive Seminars," designing them for college and university students.[52] It hired a TV performer, Janet Greene, to sing conservative folk songs at its events. It hoped that Greene's music would appeal to younger audiences and counter the protest music associated with the counterculture. Greene had starred in a local TV children's show in Ohio before an encounter with Schwarz converted her to the anti-Communist cause. Her signature song was "Poor Left Winger," which started: "I'm just a poor left-winger / Befuddled, bewildered, forlorn / Duped by a bearded singer / Peddling his communist corn / In the café espresso / Sounds of guitars could be heard. / Twanging a plaintive folk song / Spreading the communist word / Hair hung around his shoulders / And sandals were on his feet / His shirttail was ragged and dirty / Making the picture complete."[53] The song may seem a caricature, and the music was more

---

50. Ibid., 6.

51. Ibid., 4.

52. On the schools, see *Beating the Unbeatable Foe*, 382–386; and, CACC Newsletters for 16 May 1966, http://www.schwarzreport.org/uploads/schwarz-report-pdf/schwarz-report-1966-05-16.pdf (accessed 2 August 2010); and 14 November 1966, http://www.schwarzreport.org/uploads/schwarz-report-pdf/schwarz-report-1966-11-14.pdf (accessed 2 August 2010).

53. See CACC Newsletters for October 1964; http://www.schwarzreport.org/uploads/schwarz-report-pdf/schwarz-report-1964-10.pdf (accessed 30 July 2010); and 21 March 1966 http://www.schwarzreport.org/uploads/schwarz-report-pdf/schwarz

Lawrence Welk than Joan Baez or Bob Dylan, but Schwarz promoted it seriously. He believed that the cultural revolution of the 1960s signaled an acceleration of the moral decline and subversion. Combined with Communist success abroad, this demoralization would lead the US decline and global Communist hegemony by the early 1970s.

Despite these efforts, in late 1966 the CACC was in trouble, telling supporters that it needed $50,000 a month to run its programs in the US and abroad.[54] Newsletters emphasized fundraising. "We are a voluntary, nongovernmental, educational organization on a foundation of Christian love," Schwarz explained. "Our ammunition is running low, and I am compelled to appeal for generous contributions." The newsletter opened with a familiar call to arms to fight Communism in its new guise, but the undercurrent was anxiety about declining support.[55] In "1968, the receipts of the Christian Anti-Communism Crusade were less than half of their 1961 value."[56]

By the late 1960s, then, anti-Communist organizations like the CACC had lost support in measurable ways. The media paid little attention to them, no longer perceiving them as a significant a threat to mainstream America and democracy. And they no longer generated enough revenue to support their programs. The fracturing of the Democratic Party, the impact of the New Left, counterculture, anti-war movements, Black Power, and women's rights, assassinations and rioting, the populist racial politics of George Wallace, and the success of Richard Nixon and the Republican Party in 1968 and 1972—all of these had pushed organizations like the CACC to the side. The larger movement that sectarian groups like CACC represented continued to grow, nonetheless. Far right conservatives turned to organizing in the Republican Party, locally and nationally, purifying it of liberals and moderates in the 1970s and 1980s, making it increasingly

---

-report-1966-03-21.pdf (accessed 30 July 2010); See 4 April 1966 for "Poor Left Winger"; http://www.schwarzreport.org/uploads/schwarz-report-pdf/schwarz-report-1966-04-04.pdf (accessed 30 July 2010). For more material on Green, also see: http://www.conelrad.com/media/atomicmusic/sh_boom.php?platter=26; http://blog.wfmu.org/freeform/2006/01/janet_greene_th.html; and http://www.atomicplatters.com/more.php?id=119_0_1_0_M.

54. See the CACC newsletter for 17 October 1966, http://www.schwarzreport.org/uploads/schwarz-report-pdf/schwarz-report-1966-10-17.pdf (accessed 2 August 2010).

55. See the newsletter for April 8, 1967 http://www.schwarzreport.org/uploads/schwarz-report-pdf/schwarz-report-1967-04-03.pdf (accessed 3 August 2010).

56. Wilcox, "Popular Backing for the Old Christian Right," 119.

ideologically and culturally conservative in the 1990s and 2000s.[57] Scholars, journalists, and establishment Republicans were surprised by the scope and influence of groups like the CACC in the early 1960s. They would be surprised again in the late 1970s and 1980s, with the formation of the Moral Majority, which helped to elect the optimistically anti-Communist Ronald Reagan in 1980 and evolved into the Christian Coalition in the 1990s. And surprised again, in early twenty-first century, with the rise of the Tea Party and Donald Trump's successful appeal to various sectarian manifestations of the far right in his 2016 run for the presidency.

Conclusions

The buttoned-down, bow-tied Schwarz lived to see and support the Moral Majority and Christian Coalition, but not the Tea Party. He might have rejected the noisy political theater of the Tea Party (which, perhaps ironically, perhaps not, emulates the counter-culture and New Left in form); he would have been more careful in his public pronouncements than much of the religious right today; and he would have distanced himself from the racial nationalism of the "alt-Right."[58] But he would have taken advantage of twenty-first-century online and multimedia digital communication, much as he and the CACC had done with print, radio, and TV in the 1950s and 1960s. And, he would have recognized in the conflicts of our time a familiar enemy. Indeed, Schwarz's analysis in *The Three Faces of Revolution* pointed ahead to the concerns of the Right in the "culture wars" in the 1990s.[59]

---

57. See Geoffrey Kabaservice, *Rule and Ruin: The Downfall of Moderation and the Destruction of the Republican Party, From Eisenhower to the Tea Party* (New York: Oxford University Press, 2012).

58. On the alt-right, see Oliver Willis, "What Is the 'Alt-Right'? A Guide to the White Nationalist Movement Now Leading Conservative Media," *Media Matters*, 25 August 2016, http://mediamatters.org/blog/2016/08/25/what-alt-right-guide-white-nationalist-movement-now-leading-conservative-media/212643 (accessed 27 August 2016). From the right itself, see Allum Bokhari and Milo Yiannopoulos, "An Establishment Conservative's Guide to the Alt-Right," *Breitbart*, 29 March 2016, http://www.breitbart.com/tech/2016/03/29/an-establishment-conservatives-guide-to-the-alt-right/ (accessed 27 August 2016). Finally, see Michelle Goldberg, "How the 'Hipster Nazis' of the Alt Right Got Big Enough for Hillary Clinton to Denounce Them," *Slate*, 25 August 2016, http://www.slate.com/articles/news_and_politics/politics/2016/08/why_hillary_clinton_is_talking_about_donald_trump_and_the_alt_right.html (accessed 27 August 2016).

59. See James Davidson Hunter's classic, *Culture Wars: The Struggle to Define America* (New York: Basic, 1991); and Andrew Hartman's recent survey, *A War for the Soul*

David Noebel, to whom Schwarz eventually passed the torch in the CACC, recently produced a new version of a Schwarz classic, renaming it slightly: *You Can Still Trust the Communists . . . To be Communists (Socialists and Progressives Too)*.[60] For their part, opponents view the Tea Party and related "far right" or "extreme" groups as fascist threats to democracy and American values, much like liberals and the left viewed the CACC, JBS, and other militant anti-Communist organizations in the 1960s.

The rise and decline of the CACC thus echoes in the evolution and cycles of conservative militancy and the Republican Party since the 1960s. Populist activists in sectarian organizations and movements from the JBS and CACC to the Tea Party have thrived at the margins of the Republican Party, seeking influence at the center but doubting whether the Republican establishment is ever "right" enough. Occasionally sectarians have wielded influence at the center of the national party, as in the Goldwater campaign in 1964, Congressional elections in 2010, 2012 and 2014, and in the Trump campaign in 2016. They have been more consistently influential in state politics. It remains to be seen what Trump's victory and his presidency will mean. It is populist-nationalist rather than ideologically consistent. Anti-establishment militants and establishment conservative Republicans have tried to use each other, both sides ambivalent about the role ideological purists in the Party. But whether at the margins or at the center, the CACC and its kin have successfully pushed the Republican Party to the right.[61]

In short, however quirky or quaint it seems, the story of Fred Schwarz and the CACC is a window into larger histories. It is a reminder of long continuities in conservative religious and political ideas, popular culture, and organizing in the US in the twentieth and twenty-first century. And it reminds us of the role played by Californians in the emergence of the far right and of the inter-related nature of the history of California to the larger

---

of America: A History of the Culture Wars (Chicago: University of Chicago Press, 2015). Also useful is Daniel T. Rodgers, *The Age of Fracture* (Cambridge, MA: Belknap, 2012).

60. Noebel and Schwarz, *You Can Still Trust the Communists . . . To Be Communists (Socialists and Progressives Too)*, 2nd ed. (Manitou Springs, CO: Christian Anti-Communist Crusade, 2010). For the CACC's current website, go to https://schwarzreport.org/.

61. See Kabaservice, *Rule and Ruin*. See also Robert Harris, *America's Right: Anti-Establishment Conservatism from Goldwater to the Tea Party* (Malden, MA: Policy, 2013). Note also, Hemmer, *Messengers of the Right*, which focuses on the period from the 1950s to the 1970s, but makes connections to the present. See also Hemmer, "The Three Books That Shook Conservative Media in 1964," *The Atlantic*, 20 May 2016, http://www.theatlantic.com/politics/archive/2014/05/the-three-books-that-shook-conservative-media-and-politics-in-1964/371264/ (accessed 27 August 2016).

nation and the wider world. It should be no surprise that Schwarz ended up in Long Beach and that the CACC played such a prominent role in the furor over anti-Communism and the "far right" in the late 1950s and early 1960s. Southern California had been a hotbed of conservative religious and political organizing, and an evangelical media center, since the early twentieth century.

Schwarz's autobiography, *Beating the Unbeatable Foe*, proudly includes a letter sent to him by former President Reagan on the occasion of a testimonial dinner held for Schwarz in January 1990, as Communism was collapsing in eastern Europe. "Fred, you're to be commended for your tireless dedication in trying to ensure the protection of freedom and human rights," Reagan wrote, "and I know that you join me in special satisfaction in the recent events in Eastern Europe."[62] The two men had worked together against Communism in the early 1960s, crossing paths most notably at Southern California School of Anti-Communism in the later summer of 1961. Reagan was always more avuncular and pragmatic than the dogmatic, prickly Schwarz, and he believed that the US had defeated Communism and won the Cold War in a way that the conspiracy-minded Schwarz never did. To the end of his life, for example, Schwarz did not believe that China's turn to globalization signaled a rejection of Communism. He would see the devious Communist dialectic at work in China's rising global power today and in nostalgia for the Soviet era in Vladimir Putin's Russia. If not close friends, and however temperamentally different, the two men were conservative fellow travelers who found their way to Southern California and promoted the conservative side in conflicts that continue to shape American political culture today, a shared history Reagan remembered and affirmed in his letter to a grateful Schwarz.

---

62. See *Beating the Unbeatable Foe*, xx.